Discovering Your Personality Type

The Enneagram Questionnaire

Don Richard Riso

Houghton Mifflin Company

Boston · New York · London

1992

For information about bulk purchases, please see the last
page of this book.

This book contains Version 1.0 of the *Riso Enneagram Type
Indicator* (released March 1992). Subsequent editions will
contain revised versions of the RETI, as indicated by ongoing
research and testing.

Library of Congress Cataloging-in-Publication Data

Riso, Don Richard.
    Discovering your personality type : the enneagram
questionnaire / Don Richard Riso.
        p.   cm.
    ISBN 0-395-61157-1
    1. Riso Enneagram Type Indicator.   2. Enneagram.
I. Title.
BF698.8.R45R57   1992   91-43162
155.2'6 — dc20   CIP

Printed in the United States of America

BP 10 9 8 7 6 5 4 3 2 1

Line drawings by Mark Desveaux

Book design by Joyce Weston

Discovering Your Personality Type

BOOKS BY DON RICHARD RISO

Personality Types: Using the Enneagram for Self-Discovery

Understanding the Enneagram: The Practical Guide to
Personality Types

Discovering Your Personality Type:
The Enneagram Questionnaire

and the forthcoming
Working with the Enneagram:
Transforming the Personality Types

Contents

For Chalfont

Acknowledgments

WHEN I began writing about the Enneagram, one of my hopes was that publishing books about this wonderful subject would bring me into contact with wonderful people. That hope has come true, and I have been blessed not only with a life's work that seems to me to be well worth doing, but with extraordinary people with whom to do it.

I have, first of all, to thank those who have come to my Enneagram Workshops and Enneagram Teacher Training programs for their enthusiastic support. They are spreading word of the Enneagram quite literally around the world. I also want to thank those who have encouraged me to develop a questionnaire. This was not something I was interested in doing until I began to appreciate the usefulness of such an instrument. Readers and students alike can perhaps take satisfaction in knowing that they have played an important role in bringing this project about.

Ruth Hapgood, senior editor at Houghton Mifflin, continues to be a wise and steady presence. I am indebted to her for her unflagging support of my work. Thanks also to her able assistant, Sue Tecce, for seeing to the thousand details involved in producing a book. The excellence of her work is appreciated. I am grateful to Barbara Flanagan, my manuscript editor, for her sensitive and insightful suggestions. To Steve Lewers, vice-president of Houghton Mifflin, go thanks for his interest in the Enneagram and in my efforts.

I am especially indebted to Phyllis and Gary Cloninger, owners of Enneagram Designs, for their enthusiastic response to my work. Their beautiful products are a superb way to introduce the Enneagram to friends and strangers alike. Best of all, making these products available to the public was the occasion for becoming friends with these wonderful people.

In a similar vein, I would like to acknowledge Rose Mary, Ryan, Regan, Patrick, and Brett O'Boyle, Ruben St. Germain, Charles Aalto, Geoff Edholm, Rick Horton, and Anthony Cassis for their love and support.

Special thanks go to two of my students who are clinical psychologists, Quentin Dinardo, Ph.D., and Betsey Bittlingmaier, Ph.D., for their pretesting and critique of this questionnaire.

One of my most important discoveries of the last year has been my new assistant, Russ Hudson. A talented young man whose contributions to this book are too many to enumerate, Russ has helped me sharpen ideas and has suggested many new ones. I look forward to extraordinary new insights into the Enneagram when Russ begins writing about it himself.

Acknowledgment goes to my mother, Beverly Moreno Pumilia, and my father, Leo Riso, for all that they have given to me. Finally, my adviser, Brian Lawrence Taylor, is invaluable in more ways than I can say. His commitment to my work has been deep and abiding; without his constant support and guidance, doing it would have been impossible.

PART·ONE

PLEASE NOTE!
If you would like to take the *Riso Enneagram Type Indicator* right away, go to page 28 in this book now. It is not necessary to know anything about the Enneagram (pronounced "ANY-a-gram") to obtain valid results from this questionnaire.

1. A Brief Introduction to the Enneagram

Understanding Ourselves and Others

What does the Enneagram have to do with you? Why will you find it extremely worthwhile to learn about this system of personality types?

The answer is that the Enneagram is extraordinarily useful *because it works.* It is the clearest, most accurate method available for understanding ourselves and those who are important to us. It helps us understand why we do not easily get along with certain people while with others we instantly feel that we are old friends. Understanding the Enneagram is like having a pair of special glasses that allows us to see beneath the surface of people with amazing clarity: we may in fact see them more clearly than they see themselves.

The insight the Enneagram gives us can change our lives, and those who have gotten to know it cannot imagine how they once got along without it. It is as if they had been born color-blind and were suddenly able to comprehend the world in all its subtle hues for the first time. They are thrilled to uncover what had been "right in front of their noses" all along but was obscure and hidden from view. The Enneagram opens up whole new vistas for us, new depths of comprehension, new levels of meaning. Knowledge such as this is not obtained without paying a price, however: there can be no going back to our former blindness once we understand the Enneagram. The world, others, and we will be different forever.

Moreover, there are as many uses for the Enneagram as there are individuals who use it. Those who are in therapy or in one of the Twelve Step Programs or who are doing Inner Child work will find it an invaluable source of insight into their childhood and why they have become the people they are. Those in intimate relationships will benefit from understanding more about themselves and others since relationships depend, among other things, on honesty and trust. No relationship can work unless both parties bring sensitivity and insight to it, particularly when conflicts and misunderstandings arise. Understanding what others need, want, and fear, how others express themselves — as well as what they are afraid of expressing — is the best way to keep a relationship alive and growing. And understanding what we need, want, fear, and are afraid of expressing is the best way to keep our own psyches healthy.

Having insight into others is also an enormously valuable, practical skill. The Enneagram has begun to attract the attention of businesses and corporations looking for ways to increase their employees' productivity and, ultimately, their profitability. While the Enneagram is primarily a profound psychological and spiritual tool, it is also highly practical because its insights are so on target that they save a great deal of time and frustration for management and employees alike. The Enneagram can be used for hiring the "right" person for a particular job, for teaching executives to manage their employees more effectively, for clarifying a corporate image — a corporate "personality type," so to speak — or for building a more profitable sales force. Team building, sales, marketing, corporate communication, and conflict resolution — among its many applications — are more effective when the wisdom of the Enneagram is applied in the business world.

Naturally, however, if the Enneagram is to be used for self-understanding, for relationships, for therapy, or for business, one's personality type (and those of others) must be accurately assessed. This questionnaire, the *Riso Enneagram Type Indicator*, makes that possible for the first time. Those who are already acquainted with the Enneagram have intuitively sensed that this system works; the RETI attempts to go beyond intuition to verify the personality types empirically. If the Enneagram is to become more widely known, its intuitive validity will have to be corroborated by hard evidence. With the publication of this questionnaire, the scientific validation of the Enneagram has begun.

We must remember that while the Enneagram has many practical uses, its primary function is to help us understand who we are so that we transform ourselves by transcending our personality. In a sense, the Enneagram works by negating itself: the more clearly we see ourselves, the more we begin to move beyond personality, and the less we need the Enneagram. Unless we have already learned to move beyond ourselves, however, most of us still need the wisdom this system has to offer.

THE Enneagram was brought to the West by the Russian spiritual teacher George Ivanovitch Gurdjieff around the turn of the century and further developed by the Bolivian mystic Oscar Ichazo beginning in the 1960s. Ichazo brought the Enneagram to the United States in 1970, and, within a few years, awareness of this powerful typology quickly spread around North America. In 1975, I began developing the Enneagram in the light of modern psychology, adding my own insights and discoveries to the original body of knowledge. You can find more about the history and development of the Enneagram in Section 8.*

The early traditions begun by Gurdjieff and Ichazo were the first attempts to communicate the Enneagram to a modern audience; my efforts have been mainly to develop the descriptions of the personality types (and the underlying theory) so that the Enneagram could move beyond its early esoteric and religious origins to have the influence it deserves.

The psychology of the Enneagram is the primary use with which we are concerned: we discover our likeness in the mirror

* For more information about the history and transmission of the Enneagram and about Gurdjieff, Ichazo, and my further development of this system, see my *Personality Types* (1987) and *Understanding the Enneagram* (1990). Parenthetical references to those books are abbreviated as *PT* and *UTE* and include page numbers from them. Since these books contain full bibliographies about the Enneagram and related topics, that information has not been repeated here.

of the Enneagram, thereby gaining extraordinary insight into ourselves. What is particularly intriguing is that this ancient system anticipates many of the findings of the *Diagnostic and Statistical Manual of Mental Disorders*, third edition (revised), of the American Psychiatric Association, the *DSM*-III(R).

In *Understanding the Enneagram*, we saw that the Enneagram improves on the typologies proposed by modern psychology by its specificity, comprehensiveness, and elegance (209–29). It organizes observations about human nature by consolidating what has already been discovered as well as by suggesting new avenues for investigation. By "cleaving the diamond" of the psyche along its proper internal lines, the Enneagram presents us with the categories that we actually find in everyday life.

One of the primary things to understand about the Enneagram is that we find ourselves reflected in the whole of it. From one point of view, the personality types are metaphors for the various psychological functions operating in each of us. (See Section 6 for more on the Functions.) We develop into one of the nine personality types because our consciousness has been formed in a certain way as a result of our childhood experiences and heredity. Our basic personality type is, in a sense, as much a defense against our environment as an adaptive reaction to it. The remaining eight personality types (which we develop to greater or lesser degrees throughout our lives) represent the other potentials of our psyche and are important parts of who we are.

It is also worth realizing that this typology is not the sole province of academics — much less of the mystics, priests, or psychologists who originally developed it. The Enneagram belongs to everyone because it brings a person-centered humanism back to psychology and the focus of psychology back to human nature. Rather than concern ourselves about running rats through mazes as psychology has, we can see the mazes of illusion and self-deception down which we flee from the full awareness of being alive. Psychology must return to helping people meet the challenge of living consciously and purposefully. In this, the Enneagram can play a revolutionary role.

People all over the world are responding to the Enneagram

because they see their experience reflected in it. They are embracing it as one of the most important discoveries of their lives, something that has helped them make sense of what previously seemed impenetrably ambiguous or, worse, utterly chaotic. Once people grasp the essentials of this extraordinary system, they can participate in the endless adventure of deepening their understanding of themselves and their fellow humans. Who knows what benefits will accrue as new generations are able to draw on the wisdom of the Enneagram throughout their lives?

IN the last analysis, the Enneagram is extraordinarily valuable because it makes traveling the path of self-knowledge more sure. By helping us see our behaviors and motivations, thoughts and fears, attitudes and defenses, the Enneagram brings to light what was formerly hidden from us. It also provides a way out of our conflicts and confusions and helps us to be hopeful in moments of darkness and despair. It demonstrates that we are not alone in our struggles because, in so many unexpected ways, we are like everyone else.

The Enneagram is thus a *microcosm* of each of us because it provides us with a map of our development. It is also a *macrocosm* that displays the fundamental number of personality types that are necessary and sufficient for the human economy. (Too few and we would be virtually identical, which we clearly are not; too many and human beings would be incomprehensible mysteries to each other. The human family would be no more than distant cousins who have little understanding of, much less compassion for, each other.)

Furthermore, the Enneagram is of immense importance because without self-knowledge, freeing ourselves from conflicts and neuroses would be virtually impossible. Once we have been drawn into neuroses, we find it increasingly difficult to choose what is best for us, so it becomes even more difficult to work our way out of our problems. We must reverse the vicious circle created by becoming trapped in our typical fixations by choosing to accept the suffering required to turn our lives around. If we do so, we find that life becomes easier because our time and energy can be used for living creatively rather than be wasted in turmoil and conflicts. We also discover that, once we are healthy, we naturally move toward *self-transcendence* — after we have made the enormous effort to prepare ourselves for that great leap of the spirit. Pointing out each type's path of self-transcendence is thus the Enneagram's most profound gift.

Moreover, having an accurate map of our psychic landscape is a supremely practical thing because most of us have not acquired the habit of introspection, nor do we belong to an authentic spiritual school that could guide us along our path. Our materialistic Western culture does not encourage taking time from daily routines to meditate or practice spiritual disciplines so that we can acquire the resources necessary for our inner journey.

Of these resources, freedom from conflicts, delusions, and fears is among the most important. Before we can go forward we need to go inward to discover a part of ourselves that is not conflicted, deluded, or fearful. By understanding the mechanical aspects of our personality (that is, our automatic, reactive, defensive patterns), we learn how to avoid them in the future. By learning nonidentification with our personality, we become free from the shackles of our personality. Therefore, the paradox of the Enneagram is this: *We study the Enneagram because it is necessary to understand how our personality operates before we can become free of it.*

In the end, the Enneagram can be thought of as a treasure map that indicates where the secret riches of the innermost self can be discovered. But the Enneagram is only a map, and it is up to us to make the journey: only we can accept the daily challenge and adventure that is our life. The Enneagram takes us merely to the threshold of spirit and freedom, transcendence and liberation, self-surrender and self-actualization. Once we have arrived at that uncharted land, we can begin to recognize our truest self, the self beyond personality, the self of essence. That self, of course, cannot be tested by a questionnaire, but only by life itself.

How the Enneagram Works

The object of this questionnaire is to identify your basic personality type; if you answer the statements in the *Riso Enneagram Type Indicator* honestly, it will do so with a high degree of reliability.

Since this book is also a brief introduction to the Enneagram, the following explanation will be helpful for beginners. As you will see, only a few simple concepts are needed to understand how the Enneagram works. This system, however, is ultimately subtle and complex, as you will appreciate the more you use it in your life. For more guidelines, consult *Personality Types* (23–46), from which this presentation has been condensed and revised, and for further clarification *Understanding the Enneagram* (24–34).

Structure

The Enneagram's structure may look complicated, although it is actually simple. It will help you understand the Enneagram if you sketch it yourself.

Draw a circle and mark nine equidistant points on its circumference. Designate each point by a number from one to nine, with nine at the top, for symmetry and by convention. Each point represents one of the nine basic personality types.

The nine points on the circumference are also connected with each other by the inner lines of the Enneagram. Note that points Three, Six, and Nine form an equilateral triangle. The remaining six points are connected in the following order: One connects with Four, Four with Two, Two with Eight, Eight with Five, Five with Seven, and Seven with One. These six points form an irregular hexagram. The meaning of these inner lines will be discussed shortly.

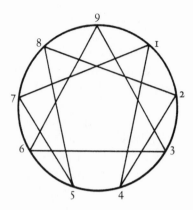

9
8   1
7   2
6   3
5   4

The Enneagram

Your Basic Personality Type

From one point of view, the Enneagram can be seen as a set of nine distinct personality types, with each number on the Enneagram denoting one type. It is common to find a little of yourself in all nine types, although one of them should stand out as being closest to yourself. This is your *basic personality type.*

Everyone emerges from childhood as *one* of the nine types, with both genetics and childhood relationships with parents or other significant persons playing an important role in the process. By the time children are four or five years old, their consciousness has developed sufficiently to have a separate sense of self. Although their identity is still very fluid, children at this age begin to establish themselves and find ways of fitting into the world on their own. Which basic personality type individuals eventually become reflects the totality of all childhood factors (including genetics) that influenced their development. (For more about genetics and the origins of each personality type, see *UTE,* 36–39.)

Several more points can be made about the basic personality type itself. First, people do not change from one basic type to another. Second, the descriptions of the personality types are universal and apply equally to males and females, since no type is inherently masculine or feminine. Third, not everything in the description of your basic type will apply to you all the time because you fluctuate constantly among the healthy, average, and unhealthy traits that make up your personality type. Fourth, the Enneagram uses numbers to designate each of the types because numbers are value-neutral — they imply the whole range of attitudes and behaviors of each type without specifying anything either positive or negative. Unlike the labels used in psychiatry, numbers provide an unbiased, shorthand way of indicating a lot about a person without being pejorative. Nor is the numerical ranking of the types significant. A larger number is no better than a smaller number; it is not better to be a Nine than a Two because nine is a higher number.

Fifth, no type is inherently better or worse than any other. While all the personality types have unique assets and liabilities, some types are often more desirable than others in any given culture or group. Furthermore, for one reason or another, you may not be happy being a particular type. You may feel that your type is "handicapped" in some way. As you learn more about all the types, you will see that just as each has unique capacities, each has different limitations. If some types are more esteemed in Western society than others, it is because of the qualities that society rewards, not because of any superior value of those types. The ideal is to become *your best self*, not to envy the assets of another type.

Identifying Your Basic Personality Type

If taken properly, the RETI will identify your basic personality type for you. This short section is included for those who want to understand the Enneagram before taking the questionnaire or for those who want to explain the Enneagram to others.

As you think about your personality, which of the following nine roles fits you best most of the time? Or, to put it differently, if you were to describe yourself in one word, which of the following words would come closest?

The Peacemaker
9

The Leader 8   1 The Reformer

The Generalist 7   2 The Helper

The Loyalist 6   3 The Motivator

The Thinker 5   4 The Artist

The Riso Enneagram Type Names

These one-word descriptors can be expanded into four-word sets of traits. Keep in mind that these are merely highlights and do not represent the full spectrum of each type.

The *Two* is caring, generous, possessive, and manipulative.
The *Three* is self-assured, ambitious, narcissistic, and hostile.
The *Four* is creative, intuitive, self-absorbed, and depressive.
The *Five* is perceptive, original, eccentric, and phobic.
The *Six* is likable, responsible, dependent, and masochistic.
The *Seven* is enthusiastic, accomplished, excessive, and manic.
The *Eight* is self-confident, decisive, dominating, and combative.
The *Nine* is receptive, reassuring, passive, and neglectful.
The *One* is rational, principled, orderly, and self-righteous.

The Triads

The Enneagram is a 3 × 3 arrangement of nine personality types *in three Triads*. There are three types in the *Feeling Triad*, three in the *Doing Triad*, and three in the *Relating Triad*, as shown below. Each Triad consists of three personality types that have in common the assets and liabilities of that Triad. For example, personality type Four has unique strengths and liabilities involving its feelings, which is why it is in the Feeling Triad. Likewise, the Eight's assets and liabilities involve its ability to relate to the environment, which is why it is in the Relating Triad, and so forth for all nine personality types.

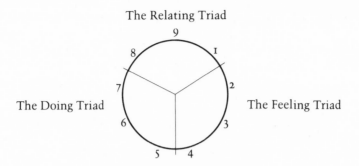

The Relating Triad

The Doing Triad   The Feeling Triad

The Triads of the Enneagram

The inclusion of each type in its Triad is not arbitrary. Each type results from a dialectic of the psychological faculty characterizing that Triad. In each Triad, one of the types overdevelops (or overexpresses) the characteristic faculty of the Triad, another type underdevelops (or underexpresses) the faculty, and the third is most out of touch (or most blocked) with the faculty. These relationships are depicted in the following illustration.

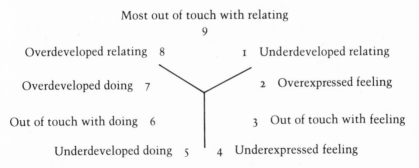

Most out of touch with relating

Overdeveloped relating   8   1   Underdeveloped relating

Overdeveloped doing   7   2   Overexpressed feeling

Out of touch with doing   6   3   Out of touch with feeling

Underdeveloped doing   5   4   Underexpressed feeling

The Dialectical Structure of the Triads

We can briefly see what this means by examining each type, Triad by Triad. In the Feeling Triad, *Twos* overexpress their feelings, excessively stating only their positive feelings for others while repressing their negative feelings (such as anger and resentment at not being appreciated enough.) *Threes* are the most out of touch with their feelings. Because they have been rewarded for their performance, they learn to project images and roles that substitute for developing genuine feelings and an inner life of their own. *Fours* underexpress their feelings since they often feel ashamed of themselves, their needs, desires, and impulses; instead of revealing themselves directly, they do so indirectly through some form of art or aesthetic living. (For more brief sketches of the types of the Feeling Triad, see *PT*, 30–31.)

In the Doing Triad, *Fives* substitute thinking for doing, so that their ability to do remains undeveloped. They find it difficult to bring closure to their quest for information and understanding and to act on what they know. Instead, they go around endlessly in ever more complex, abstract thoughts. *Sixes* are the most out of touch with their ability to act on their own without the approval or permission of an authority figure of some sort — although, ironically, Sixes also sometimes rebel against some "authorities" depending on whose values they have identified with. *Sevens* have overdeveloped their ability to act by doing things all the time. To avoid anxiety, they give in to their impulses until they become hyperactive, escapist, and manic, eventually flying out of control. (For more brief sketches of the types of the Doing Triad, see *PT*, 31–32.)

In the Relating Triad, *Eights* have overdeveloped their ability to relate to the environment because they see themselves as bigger than everyone else. They dominate everything and everyone, controlling their world so that it will conform to the way they want it to be. *Nines* are most out of touch with their ability to relate to the environment since they relate to life through an idealized vision of reality (including an idealization of other people). They are out of touch with their own sense of self because they have merged with others and have subordinated themselves to their identifications. *Ones* have underdeveloped their ability to relate to the environment in the sense that they feel themselves to be less than an ideal that they constantly strive to attain. They also feel that they must control themselves according to the dictates of their conscience, the source of their strictures on themselves and others. (For more brief sketches of the types of the Relating Triad, see *PT*, 33–34. For distinctions between the "primary" personality type and the "secondary" types, see *PT*, 26, 308–10.)

The Wing

No one is a pure personality type: everyone is a unique mixture of his or her basic type and *one* of the two types adjacent to it on the circumference of the Enneagram. One of the two types next to your basic type is your *wing*.

Your basic type dominates your overall personality, while the wing complements it and adds important, sometimes contradictory, elements to your total personality. Your wing is the "second side" of your personality, and it must be taken into consideration to better understand yourself or someone else. For example, if you are a personality type Nine, you will have *either* a One-wing or an Eight-wing, and your personality as a whole can best be understood by considering the traits of the Nine with those of either the One or the Eight as they uniquely blend in you.

There is disagreement among the various traditions of the Enneagram about whether individuals have one or two wings. Strictly speaking, everyone has two wings — in the restricted sense that both of the types adjacent to your basic type are operative in your personality since each person possesses the potentials of all nine types. However, this is not what is usually meant by "having two wings," and proponents of the so-called two-wing theory believe that both wings operate more or less equally in one's personality. (For example, they believe that a Nine would have roughly equal amounts of his or her Eight and One wings.)

Observation and testing of people leads me to conclude that the two-wing theory, like much else in the early interpretations of the Enneagram, is more intriguing than illuminating. Close observation of individuals indicates that everyone has a *dominant wing* and that while the so-called second wing always remains operative to some degree, the dominant wing is far more important. (For example, Twos with Three-wings are noticeably different from Twos with One-wings, and while Twos with

Three-wings have a One-wing, it is not nearly as important as the Three-wing.) It is therefore clearer to refer simply to a type's "wing" as opposed to its "dominant wing," since the two terms represent the same concept.

It is, of course, necessary to identify your basic type before you can assess which wing you have. In most cases, besides indicating your basic type, the *Riso Enneagram Type Indicator* will also indicate your wing. Even so, the best way to understand the influence of your wing is to read the full descriptions in *Personality Types* of the two types adjacent to your basic type and decide which best applies to you.

Directions of Integration and Disintegration

The nine personality types of the Enneagram are not static categories: they reflect our psychological growth and deterioration. The numbers on the Enneagram are connected in a sequence that denotes the Direction of Integration (health, self-actualization) and the Direction of Disintegration (unhealth, neurosis) for each personality type. In other words, as you become more healthy or unhealthy, you will move in different directions, as indicated by the lines of the Enneagram *from your basic type.*

The *Direction of Disintegration* for each type is indicated by the sequence of numbers 1-4-2-8-5-7-1. This means that if a neurotic One deteriorates further, it will be to Four; a neurotic Four will deteriorate to Two, a neurotic Two will deteriorate to Eight, a neurotic Eight to Five, a neurotic Five to Seven, and a neurotic Seven to One. (An easy way to remember the sequence is to realize that 1-4, or 14, doubles to 28, and that doubles to 57 — or almost so. Thus, 1-4-2-8-5-7 — and the sequence returns to 1 and begins again.) Likewise, on the equilateral triangle, the sequence is 9-6-3-9: a neurotic Nine will deteriorate to Six, a neurotic Six will deteriorate to Three, and a neurotic Three will deteriorate to Nine. (You can remember this sequence if you think of the numerical values diminishing as the types become more unhealthy. For a longer explanation and examples, see *PT,* 38–39.) You can see how this works by following the direction of the arrows on the following Enneagram.

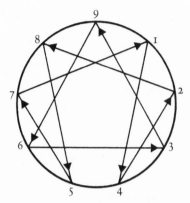

The Direction of Disintegration
1−4−2−8−5−7−1
9−6−3−9

The *Direction of Integration* for each type is indicated by the *reverse* of the sequences for disintegration. Each type moves toward integration in a direction that is the opposite of its unhealthy direction. Thus, the sequence for the Direction of Integration is 1-7-5-8-2-4-1: an integrating One goes to Seven, an integrating Seven goes to Five, an integrating Five goes to Eight, an integrating Eight goes to Two, an integrating Two goes to Four, and an integrating Four goes to One. On the equilateral triangle, the sequence is 9-3-6-9: an integrating Nine will go to Three, an integrating Three will go to Six, and an integrating Six will go to Nine. You can see how this works by following the direction of the arrows on the following Enneagram.

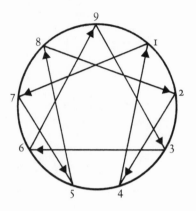

The Direction of Integration

1−7−5−8−2−4−1
9−3−6−9

It is not necessary to have separate Enneagrams for the Direction of Integration and the Direction of Disintegration. Both directions can be shown on one Enneagram by eliminating the arrows and connecting the proper points with plain lines.

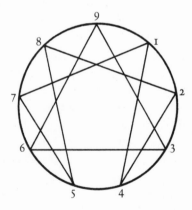

The Direction of Integration

1−7−5−8−2−4−1
9−3−6−9

The Direction of Disintegration

1−4−2−8−5−7−1
9−6−3−9

No matter which personality type you are, the types in *both* your Direction of Integration and your Direction of Disintegration are important influences. To obtain a complete picture of yourself (or of someone else), you must take into consideration the basic type and wing as well as the two types in the Directions of Integration and Disintegration. The factors represented by those *four* types blend into your total personality and provide the framework for understanding the influences operating in you. For example, no one is simply a personality type Two. A Two has either a One-wing or a Three-wing, and the Two's Direction of Disintegration (Eight) and its Direction of Integration (Four) also play important parts in his or her overall personality. (For more details, see *PT*, 39–40.)

Ultimately, the goal is for each of us to "move around" the Enneagram, integrating what each type symbolizes and acquiring the healthy potentials of *all the types*. The ideal is to become a balanced, fully functioning person who can draw on the power of each type as needed. Each of the types of the Enneagram symbolizes different important aspects of what we need to achieve this end. (See Section 6 on the Functions.) The personality type we have become is therefore ultimately unimportant; what matters is how well (or badly) we use our type as the beginning point of our self-development and self-transcendence.

The Continuum of Traits

There is an internal structure within each personality type. That structure is the Continuum of Traits (with its nine Levels of Development) which forms the personality type itself.

You have doubtless noticed that you change constantly, sometimes for the better, sometimes for the worse. Understanding the Continuum makes it clear that when you do, you are shifting within the spectrum of motivations, traits, and defenses that make up your personality type.

To understand an individual accurately, it is necessary to perceive where the person lies along the Continuum of his or her type. In other words, one must assess whether a person is healthy, average, or unhealthy to understand the person properly. This is important because, for example, two people of the same type and wing will differ significantly if one is healthy and the other unhealthy. (In relationships and in the business world, understanding this distinction is crucial.)

The Continuum for each of the personality types can be seen in the following diagram. The Continuum is composed of nine internal Levels of Development. (Briefly, there are three Levels in the healthy section, three Levels in the average section, and three Levels in the unhealthy section.) It may help you to think of the Continuum as a photographer's gray scale which has gradations from pure white to pure black with many shades of gray in between. On the Continuum, the healthiest traits appear first, at the top, so to speak. As we regress down the Continuum, we progressively pass through each Level of Development marking a distinct shift in our personality's deterioration to the pure black of psychological breakdown at the bottom.

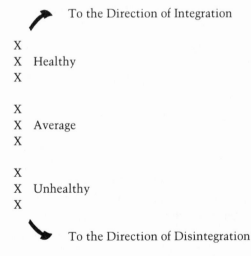

To the Direction of Integration

X
X   Healthy
X

X
X   Average
X

X
X   Unhealthy
X

To the Direction of Disintegration

The Continuum of Traits

The Continuum helps make sense of each personality type as a whole by providing a framework on which to place each healthy, average, and unhealthy trait. The Continuum is also worth understanding because it is from the healthy end that we move in the Direction of Integration, just as it is from the unhealthy end that we deteriorate to the Direction of Disintegration. This is to say that we must become healthy before we can integrate further, just as we must be neurotic before we can deteriorate into borderline states, psychosis, or schizophrenia. We simply cannot leap from neurosis to integration — or from health to instant neurosis. Integration, like disintegration, is a *process* that takes time to accomplish. We can learn to be healthy just as, in different ways and for different reasons, we learn to be unhealthy. (For more, see *PT*, 41–42, 313–18; *UTE*, 89–119.)

Typing Yourself and Others

Once you have used the *Riso Enneagram Type Indicator* to discover your type, you may be curious about the personality types of others. Since you will usually not be able to administer the RETI to business associates or to strangers, you might wonder how you can become more skilled at discovering which type someone else is. By studying the descriptions in *Personality Types* and *Understanding the Enneagram*, you will in time become more adept at typing people. As you do so, you might keep several points in mind.

You may be able to figure out the types of a few close friends rather quickly, or you may find it difficult to categorize people and not know where to begin. Either state is normal. It is not always apparent which type someone is, and it takes time and study to sharpen your skills. Remember that you are like a beginning medical student who is learning to diagnose a wide variety of conditions, some healthy, some unhealthy. It takes practice to learn to identify the various "symptoms" of each type and to see larger "syndromes."

Despite the subtleties and complexities involved, there is really no secret about typing people. You must learn which traits go with each type and observe how people manifest those traits. This is a subtle undertaking because there are many subtypes and quirks to each personality type. Different types can sometimes seem similar, particularly if their motivations are not taken into account. This is why it is not sufficient to focus on a single trait in isolation and make a diagnosis based on it alone. It is necessary to see each type as a whole — its overall style, approach to life, and especially its underlying motivations — before you can determine someone's type reliably. Many elements must come together before you can be sure that you have typed someone accurately.

Moreover, when we diagnose others, we are always on thinner ice than when we use the Enneagram to deepen our own self-knowledge. It is, of course, more appropriate to apply this material to ourselves than to type others while we avoid looking at our own lives. Nevertheless, it is unrealistic to think that anything as interesting (or as insightful) as the Enneagram will not be used to understand others. In fact, we categorize people all the time. No one approaches others without some sort of mental categories. We automatically perceive people either as male or female, attractive or unattractive, good or bad, friend or enemy, and so forth. It is not only honest to be aware of this, it is useful to have more accurate and appropriate categories for everyone, including ourselves.

Although the Enneagram is probably the most open-ended and dynamic of typologies, this does not imply that the Enneagram can say all there is to say about human beings. Individuals are understandable only up to a certain point, beyond which they remain mysterious and unpredictable. Thus, while there can be no simple explanations for persons, it is still possible to say something true about them. In the last analysis, the Enneagram helps us to do that — and only that. The Enneagram is useful because it indicates with startling clarity certain constellations of meaning about something that is essentially beyond definition: the mystery that we are.

PART·TWO

SECTION 2. Instructions

THE *Riso Enneagram Type Indicator* consists of 144 paired statements. It is a forced-choice test: it requires you to choose the statement in each pair that describes you best. In certain pairs, you may feel that neither describes you very well or, conversely, that both statements are almost equally true. Nevertheless, you must try to choose the statement that describes you *as you have been most of your life.*

Mark an X in the box to the right of the statement you have selected. For example, if you feel that a statement such as "I like oranges" fits you better than "I like apples," draw an X in the box to the right of the first statement. You may, of course, not like either oranges or apples, or you may like both. But if you were forced to choose between the two, which would you choose? Select the statement that reflects your lifelong attitudes and behavior better than the other. (If, for example, you have preferred apples most of your life but now prefer oranges, choose the apples statement.)

Be sure to choose one statement for each of the 144 pairs, taking care to put an X in the correct box. To help, a dotted line has been drawn from the end of each statement to its corresponding box in the columns on the right of the page.

You may find that there are 5 to 10 pairs of statements for which the choice is particularly difficult. The statements in the RETI are making subtle distinctions between the personality types, and choosing one over the other requires you to think carefully about which response is more true of you. In some of the pairs, both statements may *almost* be equally true. If you reflect carefully, however, you will find that one of the statements is more true than the other. Choose this statement in each pair.

Remember that there are no "right" answers. This instrument is attempting to discover your basic personality type, and if several of your selections are actually "wrong," they will not, in general, invalidate the test. So-called incorrect responses will more likely occur with factors other than those involving your basic personality type. This is why the degree of falsification they introduce in the test will be relatively small. To ensure the test's overall validity, however, it is essential that you answer honestly and thoughtfully, choosing the statement in each pair that accurately reflects your attitudes and feelings over most of your life. You must also take care to choose one of the statements in all 144 pairs; omitting several because you find them too difficult may seriously skew the results. Furthermore, the RETI is not attempting to ascertain whether or not you are healthy or unhealthy. A diagnosis such as this is beyond the scope of this test.

You may want to skip particularly difficult pairs and return to them after you have finished the entire test. Or you may wish to review your choices for the whole test after you have gone through it once. Feel free to change an original response if, after further reflection, you feel that another response is more appropriate. Naturally, you must guard against attempting to "fix" the results toward one type or another. But, because of nervousness, resistance, or other factors, you may not be able to answer some of the questions on a first pass through the test. If so, please review your responses.

The profile you get from the RETI will reflect your personality's principal psychological functions, the balance of which changes over time. While your basic personality type will remain the same, other personality functions shift as you grow, deteriorate, change attitudes, experience stress, and so forth. You may find it informative to take the RETI on several occasions to see what changes (if any) occur in your profile. If you have difficulty discovering your type because two or more top scores are very close, you might also find it helpful to discuss your choices with someone who knows you well, such as a spouse, close friend, or therapist. You may also ask someone else to take the RETI for you as an external observer, answering the questions as he or she sees you. This approach, from the point of view of how others see us, can be particularly illuminating. Several scoring sheets have been provided at the end of the test (Section 4) so that you or others can take it on different occasions. Taking and grading the RETI will require approximately one hour.

After you have taken the *Riso Enneagram Type Indicator*, read the corresponding short Profiles of your type and wing provided in Section 5 to confirm your results. (Also see *Personality Types* and *Understanding the Enneagram* for more information and complete descriptions.)

Remember that the primary goal of this test is to determine your basic personality type; in some cases, it may be necessary to interpret the results to account for unusual findings. For guidelines about interpreting the RETI, see Section 6. Again, remember to choose statements based on how you have felt and behaved **most of your life.**

3. The Riso Enneagram Type Indicator

	A	B	C	D	E	F	G	H	I
1. One of my greatest assets is the depth of my feelings		(X)							
One of my greatest assets is the sharpness of my mind			( )						
2. Although I know how to relax, I am basically hard-driving.									( )
Although I can be ambitious, I am basically easygoing.					(X)				
3. I feel good about having people depend on me									(X)
I feel uncomfortable when people depend on me		( )							
4. Others would say that I am poised and self-contained								( )	
Others would say that I am vivacious and uninhibited						(X)			
	A	B	C	D	E	F	G	H	I

SUBTOTAL

	A	B	C	D	E	F	G	H	I
5. I realize that I sometimes fret about my problems to much. . . .	(N)								
I realize that I sometimes avoid thinking about my problems too much. . . .					( )				
6. I tend to be sympathetic and to accept what people tell me about themselves. . . .									(K)
I tend to be skeptical and don't believe every story I hear. . . .						(D)			
7. Why focus on the negative when there is so much that's wonderful about life?. . . .						(N)			
I don't like being critical, but I can't help noticing when things are wrong. . . .					( )				
8. I care less about practical results than about pursuing my inspirations. . . .				(N)					
I am practical-minded and want my work to have concrete results. . . .									( )
9. I don't like to admit it, but I get into other people's business more than I should . . .									(0)
I don't like to admit it, but I let little problems go until they become big ones. . . .					(N)				
	A	B	C	D	E	F	G	H	I

SUBTOTAL

	A	B	C	D	E	F	G	H	I
10. Under pressure, I tend to detach emotionally and "go into my head"			( )						
Under pressure, I tend to worry and react strongly	(X)								
11. I am adaptable and can quickly find a way to fit into almost any situation							(X)		
I stand back from new situations and it takes me a while to see if I fit in			( )						
12. I need people to be close to me and show me affection									(X)
I want to maintain a certain distance with people			( )						
13. There's a bit of the story-teller and entertainer in me						(X)			
There's a bit of the teacher and crusader in me					(X)				
14. Although I sometimes complain about it, I need pressure to get me going	(X)								
I don't handle pressure well, and work best at my own pace					( )				
	A	B	C	D	E	F	G	H	I
SUBTOTAL									

	A	B	C	D	E	F	G	H	I

15. Much of my success has been due to my talent for making a favorable impression . . . . (x) [G]
Much of my success has been achieved despite my limited interpersonal skills . . . . ( ) [C]

16. I persuade people with my confidence and the strength of my personality . . . . ( ) [I]
I persuade people with my honesty and the reasonableness of my arguments . . . . (x) [D]

17. I worry that I will not live up to my potential . . . . (x) [G]
I worry that I'll miss out on the good things of life . . . . ( ) [F]

18. I watch people until I am sure they can be trusted . . . . . . ( ) [A]
I am very open to people and am surprised if they turn out different from what I thought . . . . (x) [E]

19. People would describe me as diplomatic, charming, and ambitious . . . . (x) [G]
People would describe me as direct, formal, and idealistic . . . . ( ) [C]

	A	B	C	D	E	F	G	H	I
SUBTOTAL									

	A	B	C	D	E	F	G	H	I
20. I brood about my problems until I can let them go		(X)							
I distract myself with other things until I find a way to handle my problems..........						( )			
21. I can assume leadership if need be, although I have problems making decisions....	( )								
It's easy for me to assume leadership and I have little problem making decisions								(X)	
22. I am romantic and give myself to many strong emotions.....		(X)							
I am logical and don't like getting too emotional				( )					
23. I am a "stormy" person and have volatile feelings..........							(X)		
I am a "mellow" person in whom "still waters run deep"..........					( )				
24. I spend my time with the interpersonal and the emotional..........									(X)
I spend my time with the abstract and the mental			( )						
25. People would say that I am often "uptight"..........	( )								
People would say that I am often "spaced out"..........					( )				
	A	B	C	D	E	F	G	H	I
SUBTOTAL									

	A	B	C	D	E	F	G	H	I
26. In general, I put practical results over abstract "ideals". In general, I put my ideals over obtaining practical "results".				(')				⊠	
27. When I am unsure of what to do, I like to get advice from others. When I need to make a decision, I try different things to see what works best for me.	⊠					( )			
28. I realize that I can sometimes be rather gushy and sentimental. I realize that I can sometimes be rather aloof and superior.							( )		⊠
29. I lose track of time and work best with as little structure as possible. I am very conscious of time and need structure to get things done.			( )		⊠				
30. I don't mind revealing my weaknesses to others, and often do. I don't want to reveal my weaknesses to others, and rarely do.		⊠						( )	
	A	B	C	D	E	F	G	H	I
SUBTOTAL									

	A	B	C	D	E	F	G	H	I

31. One of my deepest drives
is to understand the world
around me...................... ( ) *(C)*
One of my deepest drives is
to feel close to others .... (X) *(E)*

32. Unfortunately, my health
problems probably come from
worrying too much........... ( ) *(I)*
Unfortunately, my health
problems probably come from
going to extremes with my
bad habits................... (X) *(F)*

33. If I had to choose between
my career and my friends, I'd
choose my career .... ( ) *(G)*
If I had to choose between my
friends and my career, I'd
choose my friends .... (X) *(A)*

34. I hesitate to act until I've
thought through things
carefully .... ( ) *(C)*
I act quickly, confident that I
can make things work out .... (X) *(H)*

35. When I run into difficulties,
I change my tactics........... (X) *(G)*
When I run into difficulties,
I try harder................... ( ) *(D)*

	A	B	C	D	E	F	G	H	I
SUBTOTAL									

	A	B	C	D	E	F	G	H	I
36. In general, I am past-oriented		( )							
In general, I am future-oriented						✗)			
37. I don't want to see people suffer, so I usually jump in and help									✗
I don't want to spoil people, but if they want to help themselves, I'll show them how								( )	
38. I would sacrifice a great deal to be an expert in some field...			( )						
I would sacrifice a great deal to build a secure life for myself and my loved ones	✗								
39. I like "letting go" and pushing the limits							( )		
I find I don't like losing control of myself very much ...					✗				
40. I feel I have to make an effort to get people to like me .									( )
People seem to naturally like me........................					✗				
41. I am like the weather: I change constantly.............						✗			
I am like a rock: I'm solid and steady.....................								( )	
	A	B	C	D	E	F	G	H	I
SUBTOTAL									

	A	B	C	D	E	F	G	H	I

42. I distrust authority and ignore rules as much as possible.................... ( ) *[C]*
It makes me furious when others break the rules and get away with it .... ( ) *[A]*

43. I usually sympathize with the other person's point of view........................... ( ) *[F]*
Being sympathetic is okay, but others have to take responsibility for themselves........................... ( ) *[H]*

44. I have a poetic sensibility, although that usually includes feeling lonely and emotionally vulnerable.................... ( ) *[C]*
I am practical and have many new ideas, although I don't complete as many as I would like to...................... ( ) *[G]*

45. I like to share intimacies and adventures with my friends....................... ( ) *[I]*
I like to relax and unwind with friends...................... ( ) *[E]*

46. Fulfilling social obligations is not high on my agenda......... ( ) *[C]*
I take my social obligations very seriously............... ( ) *[A]*

	A	B	C	D	E	F	G	H	I
SUBTOTAL									

	A	B	C	D	E	F	G	H	I
47. I am more likely to flatter someone									( )
I am more likely to criticize someone.			( )						
48. I am "free-spirited" and don't like being attached to a lot of material things									( )
I am earthy and I enjoy dealing with the material world								( )	
49. I am more hard-working and responsible than many of my friends	( )								
I am more positive and enthusiastic than many of my friends							( )		
50. One of my main assets is my ability to describe internal states			( )						
One of my main assets is my ability to take charge of situations									( )
51. People come to me because I have knowledge that they need			( )						
People come to me because I make them feel safe and appreciated					( )				
	A	B	C	D	E	F	G	H	I
SUBTOTAL									

	A	B	C	D	E	F	G	H	I
52. It really bothers me when others don't think well of me							(·)		
I don't care if others like me as long as they respect me								( )	
53. I can be rather Spartan and need minimal creature comforts while I'm working			(.)						
It is important for me to be comfortable while I'm working							( )		
54. I feel that others will think less of me if I am not distinguishing myself in some way							( )		
I feel that I am slacking off if I am not making progress			( )						
55. I make sure that I take time to rest and reflect									( )
I don't like wasting time "doing nothing"							( )		
56. I tend to procrastinate and do not like taking the initiative myself	( )								
I take the initiative and don't mind pushing to get what I want								( )	
	A	B	C	D	E	F	G	H	I
SUBTOTAL									

	A	B	C	D	E	F	G	H	I

57. It's important to me to let others know how I feel, though I may express myself indirectly .... ( ) [B]
It's not always important to me to tell others how I feel .... ( ) [F]

58. I am an outgoing, sociable person........................... ( ) [G]
I am an earnest, self-disciplined person .... ( ) [E]

59. I am sometimes possessive of loved ones — I have trouble letting them be.................. ( ) [I]
I am sometimes ambivalent toward loved ones — pushing them away when I want them close.................. ( ) [A]

60. I tend to be confronta- tional...................... ( ) [H]
I tend to be self-effacing ..... ( ) [F]

61. It's important for me to have an aesthetically pleas- ing environment.............. ( ) [B]
Having an aesthetically pleasing environment is not a high priority for me .... ( ) [C]

A	B	C	D	E	F	G	H	I

SUBTOTAL

	A	B	C	D	E	F	G	H	I

62. A prime motive for me is to become more outstanding and esteemed as an individual................................ ( ) [G]
A prime motive for me is to become more powerful and influential as an individual........................ ( ) [H]

63. I get mad when others take for granted what I've done for them.............................. ( ) [I]
I get mad when others do not follow my instructions more carefully .... ( ) [D]

64. I need to make my own way and have trouble cooperating with others .... ( ) [G]
I need to know what is expected of me and have trouble striking out on my own.............. ( ) [A]

65. When I meet people, I come across as having a sunny, casual disposition .... ( ) [E]
When I meet people, I come across as having a mature, dignified nature.................. ( ) [D]

	A	B	C	D	E	F	G	H	I
SUBTOTAL									

	A	B	C	D	E	F	G	H	I
66. A lot of thankless tasks fall on my shoulders — I wish others would think of me for a change..........									( )
I sometimes hold myself back too much and am blocked from doing good things for myself..........		( )							
67. I identify strongly with others and form lasting bonds of trust and friendship..........	( )								
I champion others and use my resources to help them make something of themselves..........								( )	
68. I seek stimulation and excitement..........							( )		
I seek contentment and "peace of mind"..........					( )				
69. In relationships, I expect to take care of others more than they take care of me..........									( )
In relationships, I expect others to support me in my endeavors..........								( )	
70. In the face of adversity, I tend to escape into fantasy..........		( )							
In the face of adversity, I tend to "gut it out" to the bitter end..........	( )								
	A	B	C	D	E	F	G	H	I
SUBTOTAL									

	A	B	C	D	E	F	G	H	I
71. It's difficult for me to ask for things			( )						
I usually make my needs known...........................						( )			
72. I tend to be a warm, cheerful person who enjoys the company of others............									( )
I tend to be a serious, reserved person who likes discussing issues				( )					
73. I spend much of my time developing my talents and capacities							( )		
I spend much of my time in self-exploration.............			( )						
74. Whether you like it or not, you have to take care of Number One first...........								( )	
Those who think only of themselves first will end up lonely and unhappy					( )				
75. I tend to be a regular guy or gal and a traditionalist in many areas of my life	( )								
I tend to be unconventional and idiosyncratic in many areas of my life			( )						
	A	B	C	D	E	F	G	H	I
SUBTOTAL									

	A	B	C	D	E	F	G	H	I
76. I think that I am more person-oriented than goal-oriented................									( )
I think that I am more goal-oriented than person-oriented.							( )		
77. I stand by my friends, even if they might be wrong.......	( )								
I will not compromise myself for friendship................				( )					
78. When things get to me, I make it up to myself by "going on a binge"...........							( )		
When things get to me, I am able to "tune them out"......					( )				
79. Life can be ambiguous, but with insight you can begin to make sense of it all............				( )					
Life is a struggle, but with courage you can do something great................									( )
80. I am sometimes hostile and dismissive................							( )		
I am sometimes stubborn and defensive	( )								
81. I let others find their own way and make their own mistakes................			( )						
I think it's better to help others see that they are making a mistake					( )				
	A	B	C	D	E	F	G	H	I
SUBTOTAL									

	A	B	C	D	E	F	G	H	I

82. I use my money primarily to maintain and improve my position in life . . . . ( ) [H]
   I use my money primarily to obtain interesting, pleasurable experiences . . . . ( ) [E]

83. I am self-conscious about how I come across to people . . . . ( ) [G]
   I am not particularly self-conscious when I am around people . . . . ( ) [E]

84. I am patient: I stand back and observe things . . . . ( ) [C]
   I am impatient: I jump in and attack problems . . . . ( ) [D]

85. I often counsel people and give personal advice . . . . ( ) [I]
   I don't get too personally involved in other people's lives . . . . ( ) [A]

86. I usually feel like an outsider . . . . ( ) [B]
   I usually feel comfortable around people . . . . ( ) [F]

	A	B	C	D	E	F	G	H	I
SUBTOTAL									

	A	B	C	D	E	F	G	H	I
87. It's hard for me not to complain when others don't do their jobs and put me under more pressure	( )								
It's hard for me not to put down those who can't keep up with my pace						( )			
88. Privately, I think I am better than most.								( )	
Privately, I think I am more flawed than most.		( )							
89. I often go too far and make myself too emotionally available to people.									( )
It's hard for me to let down my guard around people — even my loved ones.								( )	
90. People have said that I'm too argumentative — I guess I enjoy a good debate.			( )						
People have said that I'm too accommodating — I just don't like arguing.							( )		
91. I may seem to others to be self-indulgent and sensual		( )							
I may seem to others to be impersonal and self-controlled				( )					
	A	B	C	D	E	F	G	H	I
SUBTOTAL									

	A	B	C	D	E	F	G	H	I
92. I am well disciplined: I know how to get organized and follow through with details	( )								
I am less disciplined: I know how to be spontaneous and improvise									( )
93. I realize that sometimes I am too complacent and a daydreamer					( )				
I realize that sometimes I am too judgmental and impatient				( )					
94. I don't like admitting it, but I often compare myself with others							( )		
I don't like admitting it, but I am rarely satisfied with what I have						( )			
95. I am a soft touch for those who are down on their luck									( )
There are proper channels to which a needy person can apply for help				( )					
96. Typically, when I get angry I become distant and icy							( )		
Typically, when I get angry I shout and tell people off								( )	
	A	B	C	D	E	F	G	H	I
SUBTOTAL									

	A	B	C	D	E	F	G	H	I

97. I often feel inhibited and unable to express myself well . . . . ( )
I am outspoken — I say what others wish they had the nerve to say . . . . ( )

98. I don't fear having conflicts with others . . . . ( )
I fear having conflicts with others . . . . ( )

99. I tend to be moody and self-absorbed . . . . ( )
I tend to be emotionally detached and preoccupied . . . . . ( )

100. I suppose it's true that I need to be needed — but doesn't everyone? . . . . ( )
I suppose it's true that I am self-centered and don't like people needing me too much . . . . ( )

101. I enjoy talking about myself and being the center of attention . . . . ( )
I feel uneasy talking about myself and being the center of attention . . . . ( )

	A	B	C	D	E	F	G	H	I

SUBTOTAL

	A	B	C	D	E	F	G	H	I
102. I sometimes put people off by being too forceful.........								( )	
I sometimes put people off by being too impersonal.........				( )					
103. I tend to avoid most physical activities...............			( )						
I have tended to like most physical activities.............						( )			
104. Generally speaking, I have tended to be pessimistic.........		( )							
Generally speaking, I have tended to be optimistic........					( )				
105. I prefer working to help people on a one-to-one basis........................									( )
I prefer working with others on a team effort........	( )								
106. Having people admire me is important to me...........							( )		
Having an impact on the lives of others is important to me...								( )	
107. It is hard to know what to do because morality is so relative......................			( )						
It is easy to know what to do because moral truth is objective..................				( )					
	A	B	C	D	E	F	G	H	I
SUBTOTAL									

	A	B	C	D	E	F	G	H	I
108. I depend on my friends and they know they can depend on me	( )								
I don't depend on people: I want to do things on my own							( )		
109. I am more intuitive than cerebral		( )							
I am more cerebral than intuitive			( )						
110. I have a deep need for security	( )								
I have a strong need to feel that I am right				( )					
111. I have found that the more I reduce my needs, the simpler life becomes			( )						
I have found that the more I have, the simpler life becomes								( )	
112. I am a perfectionist and I push to get things done right, even if it makes people uncomfortable				( )					
I am less perfectionistic — getting along with people is more important to me					( )				
	A	B	C	D	E	F	G	H	I

SUBTOTAL

	A	B	C	D	E	F	G	H	I
113. When I have conflicts with others, I tend to withdraw		( )							
When I have conflicts with others, I rarely back down								( )	
114. I make friends easily and often									( )
I don't make friends easily			( )						
115. I am secretive about my private life							( )		
I talk openly about my private life						( )			
116. People have told me to stop considering so many alternatives and do something definite			( )						
People have told me that I need to relax and enjoy life for a change				( )					
117. I am fairly impractical and something of a dreamer			( )						
I am practical and down-to-earth	( )								
118. I give people attention and nurturance									( )
I give people direction and motivation								( )	
	A	B	C	D	E	F	G	H	I
SUBTOTAL									

	A	B	C	D	E	F	G	H	I
119. I am methodical and cautious	( )								
I am adventurous and take risks.						( )			
120. I am ambitious and push myself to realize my dreams.							( )		
I am not very ambitious for myself, but I work hard for my loved ones					( )				
121. I tend to be focused and intense.			( )						
I tend to be spontaneous and fun-loving.						( )			
122. Generally, my actions are based on the needs of the situation								( )	
Generally, my actions are based on principles				( )					
123. It's difficult for me to tell people how special they are to me			( )						
It's easy for me to tell people how special they are to me									( )
	A	B	C	D	E	F	G	H	I
SUBTOTAL									

	A	B	C	D	E	F	G	H	I
124. The positive feedback I get from others is important to me							( )		
I know if I've done something well, and don't need the reactions of others to confirm it			( )						
125. I'm very free with money, and spend more lavishly than I should						( )			
I have worked hard for my money and keep track of it carefully								( )	
126. I know the right way to live				( )					
I know how to make something of myself							( )		
127. I am able to get others to confide in me									( )
What people do is their own business and it doesn't concern me					( )				
128. I take time to figure out what my feelings and impulses are telling me		( )							
Navel-gazing is a waste of time: getting things done is what counts								( )	
	A	B	C	D	E	F	G	H	I
SUBTOTAL									

	A	B	C	D	E	F	G	H	I
129. I function well in groups ...	( )								
I find it frustrating to function in groups				( )					
130. It makes me mad when people refuse to face unpleasant realities................				( )					
It makes me mad when people try to upset me about things I can't do anything about					( )				
131. I usually follow my feelings and impulses...............							( )		
I usually follow my conscience and reason................					( )				
132. I find I often get attached to people.....................									( )
I find I often get competitive with people.................							( )		
133. In social situations, I tend to talk intimately with one or two people or else keep to myself.....................		( )							
In social situations, I tend to talk and banter with a lot of different people............	( )								
134. I love having a lot of people in my life							( )		
I don't need a lot of people in my life.....................								( )	
	A	B	C	D	E	F	G	H	I
SUBTOTAL									

	A	B	C	D	E	F	G	H	I
135. When I get angry at people, I find it difficult to confront them		( )							
When I get angry at people, I let them know what is on my mind					( )				
136. I am emotionally demonstrative									( )
I am not very emotionally demonstrative			( )						
137. I'm not very easy to get to know — I like to keep people guessing								( )	
I'm like an open book — "what you see is what you get"					( )				
138. In a difficult situation, I need reassurance from others	( )								
In a difficult situation, I am usually sure of where I stand					( )				
139. I reach out to people									( )
I rarely reach out to people		( )							
140. I want to be socially acceptable								( )	
I care little about being socially acceptable			( )						
	A	B	C	D	E	F	G	H	I

SUBTOTAL

	A	B	C	D	E	F	G	H	I
141. I like many different things and am eager for new experiences							( )		
I know what I like, so why waste my time trying something I might not like? ...					( )				
142. One of my fears is being taken advantage of	( )								
One of my fears is being dependent on someone else ...								( )	
143. I often question myself about my motives and feelings		( )							
I seldom question myself about my motives and feelings........................					( )				
144. I don't believe that personality questionnaires are valid because they cannot encompass the unlimited potential of human beings							( )		
I believe that personality questionnaires are probably valid because human behavior is limited and rather predictable			( )						
	A	B	C	D	E	F	G	H	I
SUBTOTAL									

SECTION **4. Scoring Instructions**

A DD the X's marked in column A, column B, column C, and so forth, through column I, and enter the numbers in the corresponding boxes below. If you have marked one box in each pair of statements and have added the number of X's correctly, the sum will be 144. If not, go back and recheck for mistakes either in counting X's or in arithmetic. Each column corresponds to a personality type, as given in the chart below. Please note that the types have been randomized and are *not* in numerical order.

Columns	A	B	C	D	E	F	G	H	I
Numerical Value									
Personality Type	Six	Four	Five	One	Nine	Seven	Three	Eight	Two

Mark the numerical value for each personality type on the score sheet on page 58. Note that the personality types have been arranged on the score sheet *in numerical order* beginning with types Two, Three, Four (in the Feeling Triad), and so forth. You may wish to connect the marks you have made to produce a graph.

Except in unusual circumstances (some of which are discussed in Section 6), your highest score will indicate your *basic personality type* — which is the object of this test. To confirm your test results, read the short Profile of your basic type in Section 5 as well as the more complete descriptions in *Personality Types* and *Understanding the Enneagram*.

An alternative method for discovering your personality type is to have one or more people who know you well take the RETI as if they were answering the test for you (as mentioned in Section 2). This method tests how others see you; if their results and yours are the same (at least for the basic type), you can be reassured that the RETI has discriminated your type accurately. On the other hand, a finding of a different basic type (or of a dramatically different pattern for the other eight types) could be the basis for discussing various dimensions of your personality that you formerly may have been unaware of.

The median score is 16 for each type. If the Functions of your personality were in perfect balance, you would score 16 on each of the nine types. This result is probably extremely rare, and it is normal to have wide variations from the median. Some scores will fall below the median, some will be above it. These variations produce a profile of your personality whose imbalances represent your ever-changing responses to life. The "high normal" and "low normal" as well as the "overdeveloped" and "underdeveloped" ranges indicated on the score sheets are therefore not to be interpreted as indications of pathology or as value judgments. They are only indicators of the *relative* development of the various Functions within your personality. Thus, those Functions that are already developed probably do not need to be emphasized further, while you may want to give more attention to those that are underdeveloped.

After you have plotted your scores on the score sheet(s), read the appropriate brief Profile of your type in Section 5 and then go to Section 6 for more information about interpreting your results.

Score Sheet I

Type	Two	Three	Four	Five	Six	Seven	Eight	Nine	One	
Score										
32										
31										
30										
29										
28										
27										
26										
25										
24										Over-developed
23										
22										
21										
20										High Normal
19										
18										
17										
16										Median
15										
14										
13										
12										Low Normal
11										
10										
9										
8										Under-developed
7										
6										
5										
4										
3										
2										
1										
0										
	Two	Three	Four	Five	Six	Seven	Eight	Nine	One	
	The Feeling Triad			The Doing Triad			The Relating Triad			

Score Sheet II

Type	Two	Three	Four	Five	Six	Seven	Eight	Nine	One	
Score										
32										
31										
30										
29										
28										
27										
26										
25										
24										Over-developed
23										
22										
21										
20										High Normal
19										
18										
17										
16										Median
15										
14										
13										
12										Low Normal
11										
10										
9										
8										Under-developed
7										
6										
5										
4										
3										
2										
1										
0										
	Two	Three	Four	Five	Six	Seven	Eight	Nine	One	
	The Feeling Triad		The Doing Triad			The Relating Triad				

Score Sheet III

Type	Two	Three	Four	Five	Six	Seven	Eight	Nine	One	
Score										
32										
31										
30										
29										
28										
27										
26										
25										
24										Over-developed
23										
22										
21										
20										High Normal
19										
18										
17										
16										Median
15										
14										
13										
12										Low Normal
11										
10										
9										
8										Under-developed
7										
6										
5										
4										
3										
2										
1										
0										
	Two	Three	Four	Five	Six	Seven	Eight	Nine	One	
	The Feeling Triad			The Doing Triad			The Relating Triad			

Score Sheet IV

Type	Two	Three	Four	Five	Six	Seven	Eight	Nine	One	
Score										
32										
31										
30										
29										
28										
27										
26										
25										
24										Over-
23										developed
22										
21										
20										High
19										Normal
18										
17										
16										Median
15										
14										
13										
12										Low
11										Normal
10										
9										
8										Under-
7										developed
6										
5										
4										
3										
2										
1										
0										
	Two	Three	Four	Five	Six	Seven	Eight	Nine	One	
	The Feeling Triad			The Doing Triad			The Relating Triad			

PART·THREE

5. The Personality Types in Profile

Profiles

Now that you have discovered your personality type, you will naturally want to know more about what it means.

The following Profiles will introduce you to each of the nine personality types of the Enneagram. Remember that these Profiles are intentionally brief, impressionistic sketches and by no means exhaust the behaviors and motivations that make up each type, much less the insights that can be had about them.

Each Profile begins with a short overview of the type, then lists some of the major healthy, average, and unhealthy traits, and ends with references to *Personality Types* and *Understanding the Enneagram*. These books contain a wealth of information about each type, including full systematic descriptions, short profiles (in *PT*), expanded profiles (in *UTE*), descriptions of each type's Directions of Integration and Disintegration, its basic fear, basic desire, and secondary motivations, its developmental childhood origins, descriptions of the wings, examples of famous people (listed according to their wing), the type's sense of self, characteristic temptation, saving grace, characteristic vice and virtue, suggestions for personal growth, its abstract structural patterns, and much else. By my convention, the profiles begin with personality type Two in the Feeling Triad.

Personality Type Two: *The Helper*
The Caring, Mothering Type: Concerned, Helpful, Possessive, and Manipulative

Personality type Two is the type in the Feeling Triad that is overexpressive of its feelings. Twos demonstrate their emotions, openly declaring their love and affection for others. The problem is that while they are aware of their positive feelings for others, they are unaware of repressing their resentment toward those who are not grateful for what Twos have done for them. Twos see themselves as loving, kind, and thoughtful (and when they are healthy, they are). However, as they become unhealthy, their behavior contradicts their all-loving self-image as they desperately coerce signs of love and appreciation from others. The following are some of the major behavioral characteristics of Twos.

Healthy: They are empathetic, compassionate, feeling with and for others, caring and concerned about their needs. Encouraging, appreciative, sincere, and warm-hearted. Service is very important to Twos: they are generous, giving, and helpful — loving, thoughtful people. *At their best:* Very healthy Twos become deeply unselfish, disinterested, and altruistic: giving unconditional love. They feel it is a privilege to be in the lives of others. They are saintly and deeply humble and truly do not think of themselves.

Average: Average Twos begin to do more talking about what they will do for others than giving actual help. They become gushy, emotionally demonstrative, histrionic, overly friendly, and full of "good intentions" about everything. The attention they give is seductive: approval, "strokes," flattery, cultivating people. Love and friendship are their supreme values, and they talk about them constantly. Become overintimate and intrusive: they need to be needed, so they hover, meddle, and control in the name of love. Wanting others to depend on them, they give but expect a return. Enveloping and possessive: the self-sacrificial, mothering person who cannot do enough for others. They wear themselves out for everyone, creating needs for themselves to fulfill. They develop hypochondria, becoming "martyrs" for others. Feel increasingly self-important and indispensable, although they overrate their efforts in others' behalf. Overbearing, patronizing, and self-satisfied.

Unhealthy: They can be manipulative and self-serving, instilling guilt by telling others how much they owe them. Undermine people, making belittling, disparaging remarks. Extremely self-deceptive about their motives and about how aggressive or selfish their behavior has become. Domineering and coercive: they feel entitled to get anything they want from others — the repayment of old debts, money, sexual favors. Able to excuse and rationalize whatever they do since they feel abused and victimized and are bitterly resentful and angry. Suppression of their aggressions results in psychosomatic problems.

See *Personality Types,* 49–76, *Understanding the Enneagram,* 44–49, and "Recommendations for Personal Growth" in *UTE,* 236–38.

Personality Type Three: *The Motivator*
The Success-Oriented, Pragmatic Type: Self-Assured, Ambitious, Narcissistic, and Hostile

Personality type Three is the type in the Feeling Triad that is most out of touch with its feelings. Thus, the underlying problem with average to unhealthy Threes is that they tend to be emotionally undeveloped: they have put their energy primarily into learning how to come across to others well so that they can garner attention and admiration. Threes have learned to do what it takes to be noticed and to be in demand socially by projecting a desirable image. Because their private sense of self remains undeveloped, however, average to unhealthy Threes do not know who they are apart from the images they project. Rather than express what they actually think or feel, they say or do what will be acceptable and applauded. Some of the major behavioral characteristics of Threes are the following.

Healthy: They are self-assured, desirable, have high self-esteem, and believe in themselves and their own value. Adaptable, energetic, often physically attractive and popular. Ambitious to improve themselves, to be the best they can be: they often become outstanding, a human ideal, embodying widely admired cultural qualities. Others are motivated to be like them in some positive way. *At their best:* Self-accepting, inner-directed, and authentic, everything they seem to be. They accept their limitations and live within them.

Average: They become competitively concerned with superiority and rising above others, comparing self with others for prestige and status. They become identified with success and career, with distinguishing themselves in some way: exclusivity and social recognition are important. Pragmatic, goal-oriented, and efficient, but also calculating, becoming image-conscious, highly aware of how they appear to others. Potential problems with intimacy and honesty emerge as they package the self according to the expectations of others and doing whatever produces the desired results. As identification with performance increases, they want to impress others and have their image reinforced. They constantly promote themselves, making themselves sound better than they actually are. Narcissistic, pretentious, with grandiose expectations and pretensions. Exhibitionistic tendencies, as well as arrogance, hostility, and contempt for others surface.

Unhealthy: Fearing failure and humiliation, they can be exploitative and opportunistic, essentially out for themselves. To stay on top, they tend to use others dishonestly, to lie or steal (things, ideas, corporate information, and so on). Untrustworthy, they maliciously betray people but begin to be devious and deceptive so that their deceit and duplicity will not be exposed. Delusionally jealous of others: become vindictive, attempting to ruin others' happiness. Diabolically sadistic, psychopathic tendencies emerge as extreme form of pathology.

See *Personality Types*, 77–104, *Understanding the Ennea-gram*, 49–53, and "Recommendations for Personal Growth" in *UTE*, 239–41.

Personality Type Four: *The Artist*
The Melancholy, Withdrawn Type: Creative, Individualistic, Withdrawn, and Depressive

Personality type Four is the type in the Feeling Triad that under-expresses its feelings. Fours find their feelings difficult to express because they are powerful, mixed with sexual and forbidden ele-ments, often with negative feelings about themselves and others. Because their feelings are often shameful, chaotic, and "danger-ous," average to unhealthy Fours have learned to keep their feel-ings to themselves, partly so that they can sort them out, and partly to spare themselves from humiliation or punishment if they were to reveal how they actually feel. But as they continue to turn their feelings inward, average to unhealthy Fours become painfully self-conscious and emotionally vulnerable and suffer many far-ranging practical negative consequences in their lives and relationships. Some of the major behavioral characteristics of Fours are the following.

Healthy: Fours are self-aware, introspective, searching for self, aware of feelings and inner impulses. Intuitive and sensitive both to self and others: gentle, tactful, compassionate. Ironic view of self: can be serious and funny, vulnerable and emotionally strong. Highly personal, individualistic, true to self, self-reveal-ing, emotionally honest, and humane. *At their best:* Profoundly creative, expressing the personal and the universal, possibly in art. Inspired, self-renewing, and regenerative: able to transform all their experiences into something valuable for others as well.

Average: They take an aesthetic, artistic, romantic orientation to life, expressing personal feelings through something beauti-ful. Heighten reality and emotions through the imagination. To stay in touch with feelings, they interiorize everything, taking everything personally, becoming self-absorbed, introverted, and moody. Also become hypersensitive, shy and very self-conscious, unable to be spontaneous or to get outside themselves. They remain socially withdrawn to protect the vulnerable self and to sort out their mixed, increasingly negative feelings. They gradually feel different from others and therefore exempt from living as others do. Self-pity leads to self-indulgence, to becoming melancholic dreamers, decadent and sensual, living in a fantasy world that repels any kind of pressure or intrusion. Increasingly impractical, unproductive, effete, petulant, and precious.

Unhealthy: When their dreams and expectations fail, they become angry at themselves: self-inhibited, depressed, and alienated from self and others, incapacitated, blocked, and emotionally paralyzed. Ashamed of self, fatigued, and unable to function. Tormented by delusional self-contempt, self-reproaches, self-hatred, and morbid thoughts: everything becomes a source of torment. They despair, feel hopeless, and become self-destructive, possibly abusing alcohol or drugs to escape. In the extreme, emotional breakdown or suicide is the likely form of pathology.

See *Personality Types*, 105–33, *Understanding the Enneagram*, 53–57, and "Recommendations for Personal Growth" in *UTE*, 241–44.

Personality Type Five: *The Thinker*
The Intellectual, Analytic Type: Perceptive, Original, Eccentric, and Phobic

Personality type Five is the type in the Doing Triad that has underdeveloped its ability to do or to take practical action. Fives tend to substitute thinking for doing, feeling that they cannot risk acting until they have first carefully thought about what they might do, learned as much as possible about the task at hand, and foreseen every possible outcome if they act one way or another. Fives are caught in their heads, in thinking, since thinking about doing, feelings, and relationships is safer and less threatening than experiencing them. Fives are constantly vigilant about the world around them (particularly people) lest anyone or anything catch them by surprise and make them feel in danger of being overwhelmed. The following are some of the major behavioral characteristics of Fives.

Healthy: They observe everything with extraordinary perceptiveness and insight. Mentally alert, curious, with a searching intelligence: nothing escapes their notice. They value foresight and prediction. Able to concentrate, becoming engrossed in what has caught their attention. Excited by knowledge, they often become experts in some field. Independent, innovative, inventive, producing extremely valuable, original ideas. *At their best:* Become visionaries, broadly comprehending the world while penetrating it profoundly. Open-minded, take things in whole, in their true context. Make pioneering discoveries of something entirely new.

Average: They become specialized, analytic, highly intellectual, making a science of things: they become engrossed in reading, learning, and building theories. Speculating about abstract, complicated ideas, preoccupied with interpretations and possibilities rather than data and facts. They love details, esoteric, abstruse subjects, and lose the forest for the trees, not seeing the context. Withdrawing from the practical world, they become more detached mentally, while emotionally they become more highstrung and intense. Begin to interpret everything according to a pet theory, becoming reductionistic, farfetched, imposing ideas on the facts. Iconoclastic, provocative, extremist, radical interpretations that may contain valuable insights but also half-truths. Cynical, angry, and argumentative: others are stupid and are to be debunked and ridiculed.

Unhealthy: They become reclusive and isolated, highly antagonistic, and yet fearful of aggressions: reject and repulse all social attachments, becoming eccentric, strange. Frightened by threatening ideas, yet obsessed by them as well: they have paranoid tendencies and are prey to gross distortions and phobias. Lose touch with reality: insanity with schizophrenic tendencies is the likely form of pathology.

See *Personality Types*, 134–61, *Understanding the Enneagram*, 58–62, and "Recommendations for Personal Growth" in *UTE*, 244–46.

Personality Type Six: *The Loyalist*
The Committed, Traditionalistic Type: Likable, Responsible, Dependent, and Masochistic

Personality type Six is the type in the Doing Triad that is most out of touch with its ability to act independently of others. People of this type have little or no problem with doing, however, if their actions are sanctioned by an authority or belief system of some sort. (They may also rebel against one authority or system in the name of another.) What is crucial for Sixes is the system or person they have identified with: their sense of self depends on that identification. Average to unhealthy Sixes are prey to anxiety and insecurity when they are unsure of where they stand with others, particularly with their authority figures. Some of the major behavioral characteristics of Sixes are the following.

Healthy: Sixes are able to elicit strong emotional responses from others: very appealing, endearing, and lovable. Trust is important: bonding with others, forming permanent relationships. Committed and loyal to those with whom they have identified: family and friends important, as is the sense that they belong somewhere. Respond with reliable, responsible, trustworthy behavior. *At their best:* They become self-affirming, trusting of self and others, independent yet symbiotically interdependent and cooperative as an equal. Faith in self leads to courage, positive thinking, leadership, and rich self-expression, sometimes as an artist.

Average: They fear taking responsibility for themselves: identify with an authority figure (or a group), becoming obedient to it.

Traditionalistic and loyal to the organization, dutifully doing what they are told. However, they also react against the authority indirectly, passive-aggressively. Become evasive, indecisive, cautious, procrastinating, ambivalent. As ambivalence causes them to oscillate, they become contradictory, give mixed signals, and react unpredictably. To overcompensate for insecurities, they become highly aggressive and belligerent, taking a "tough guy," rebellious stance toward anyone they perceive as an enemy or threat to them and their identifications. In-groups and out-groups are identified, as they become highly partisan, defensive, looking for threats to their security. Mean-spirited, authoritarian, bigoted, they lash out at others to silence fears.

Unhealthy: Fearing rejection by the authority, unhealthy Sixes become insecure, clingingly dependent, and self-disparaging, with acute inferiority feelings. Feel hopeless, worthless, incompetent. Extremely anxious, they feel persecuted and believe that others are out to get them. Overreact to anxiety and problems: act irrationally and may bring about what they fear. They may choose self-defeat and humiliation to be rescued from anxiety, the fear of abandonment, and the other consequences of their actions. Masochism and various forms of self-punishment are the likely form of pathology.

See *Personality Types*, 162–89, *Understanding the Enneagram*, 63–67, and "Recommendations for Personal Growth," in *UTE*, 247–49.

Personality Type Seven: *The Generalist*
The Hyperactive, Uninhibited Type: Enthusiastic,
Accomplished, Excessive, and Manic

Personality type Seven is the type in the Doing Triad that has overdeveloped its ability to do. People of this type tend to do too much: they put no restraints on themselves as they constantly search for new experiences and sources of stimulation. They impulsively do too many things at the same time, distracting themselves by acquiring and consuming more of everything to deaden anxiety and spare themselves from the fear of being deprived. Average to unhealthy Sevens often have many material possessions and yet are unsatisfied because they cannot give themselves to anything (lest they miss out on something more desirable). Some of the major behavioral characteristics of Sevens are the following.

Healthy: They are highly responsive, excitable, enthusiastic, the most extroverted type: stimuli bring immediate responses, and they find everything invigorating. Lively, vivacious, eager, spontaneous, resilient, exhilarated. Quickly become accomplished achievers who do many things very well: they are multi-talented generalists. Practical, highly productive, prolific, cross-fertilizing their many areas of interest and skills. *At their best:* They assimilate experiences in depth, making them deeply grateful and appreciative, awed by the wonders of life: joyous and ecstatic. They have intimations of spiritual reality, of the goodness of life.

Average: As their appetites increase, they want to have more of whatever has made them happy. Become acquisitive, materialistic, worldly-wise, constantly amusing themselves with new things and experiences: sophisticate, connoisseur, collector, and consumer. Money, amusements, and variety are important. Become hyperactive, unable to say no to themselves, to deny themselves anything. Uninhibited, they throw themselves into constant activity, doing and saying whatever comes to mind: flamboyant exaggerations, storytelling, wisecracking constantly. An oral type, they talk, eat, drink, and smoke — all at the same time. Fear being bored: in perpetual motion, but into too many things, becoming superficial dilettantes merely dabbling around. Get into conspicuous consumption and all forms of excess, yet greedy for more, never feeling that they have enough. Demanding, self-centered, yet jaded and unsatisfied. Hardened and insensitive, with addictive tendencies.

Unhealthy: They can be offensive and abusive while going after what they want. Impulsive and infantile, not knowing when to stop. Addictions and excess take their toll: they become debauched, depraved, dissipated escapists. Acting out impulses rather than dealing with anxiety or frustrations: go out of control, into erratic mood swings and compulsive actions (manias). In flight from self, subject to panic reactions if defenses fail. Severe manic-depressive mood swings are the likely form of pathology.

See *Personality Types,* 190–217, *Understanding the Enneagram,* 67–71, and "Recommendations for Personal Growth" in *UTE,* 249–51.

Personality Type Eight: *The Leader*
The Powerful, Dominating Type: Self-Confident, Decisive, Dictatorial, and Destructive

Personality type Eight is the type in the Relating Triad that has overdeveloped its ability to relate to the environment. Eights typically have problems relating to people because they want to dominate whoever is in their orbit. People of this type experience themselves as people who can get what they want. While not necessarily brutal, Eights can be aggressive in an unstated fight for survival for themselves and for those they want to protect and defend. They can have either a highly beneficial effect on the environment or just the reverse. Some of the major behavioral characteristics of Eights are the following.

Healthy: Eights are self-assertive, self-confident, and strong: they have learned to stand up for what they need and want. Have a resourceful, can-do attitude and inner drive. Decisive, solid, authoritative, commanding, honorable: natural leaders, whom others look up to. Passionate, they take initiative and make things happen: champion of people, provider, protector. *At their best:* Become self-restrained and magnanimous, merciful and forbearing, mastering self, carrying others with their strength. Courageous, putting themselves in jeopardy to achieve their vision: possibly heroic and historically great.

Average: Self-sufficiency and financial independence are highly important: they become enterprising, rugged individualists, wheeler-dealers, and entrepreneurs. Love adventure, risk taking, coming out on top. Begin to want to dominate the environment completely, including others. Become forceful, aggressive, expansive: the empire builder, monarch, boss whose word is law. Proud and egocentric, they want to impose their will and vision on everything. Order others around as if chattel; do not respect others; create master-slave relationships. Tendency to mix sex, aggression, coarseness, and vulgarity. Become extremely combative and intimidating to get their way: confrontational, belligerent, creating adversarial relationships. Everything a test of wills, and they will not back down. Use threats and reprisals to extort obedience from others, to keep others off balance and powerless. Make others feel insecure, oppressed. Unjust treatment makes others fear and resent them, possibly also to band together.

Unhealthy: They can be completely ruthless: dictatorial, tyrannical, believing that "might makes right." Immoral, violent, and hardhearted. Develop delusional ideas about themselves: megalomaniacal, omnipotent, invulnerable. They overextend themselves, and if in danger themselves, they may brutally destroy everything that has not conformed to their will. Pathology is extreme antisocial behavior: vengeful, barbaric, murderous.

See *Personality Types,* 218–45, *Understanding the Enneagram,* 72–76, and "Recommendations for Personal Growth" in *UTE,* 252–54.

Personality Type Nine: *The Peacemaker*
The Easygoing, Phlegmatic Type: Accepting, Reassuring, Passive, and Repressed

Personality type Nine is the type in the Relating Triad that is most out of touch with its ability to relate to the environment as it is. People of this type have so completely identified with an idealized vision of reality or another person that they lack a sufficient sense of themselves apart from their idealizations. Nines and their idealized visions merge into one. While this gives Nines a profound sense of peace and well-being, it also exposes them to being too repressed, undeveloped, and unresponsive to reality. Rather than deal with anything that upsets them by contradicting their idealized vision, average to unhealthy Nines ignore what they do not want to see. The following are some of the major behavioral characteristics of Nines.

Healthy: They are deeply accepting, receptive, unself-conscious, emotionally stable and serene. Innocent and simple, they are trusting of self and others, at ease with self and life. Patient, unpretentious, good-natured, genuinely nice people. Optimistic, reassuring, supportive: a calming influence — harmonizing groups, bringing people together. Good mediator, sustainer, comforter. *At their best:* They become self-possessed, feeling autonomous and fulfilled: have great equanimity and contentment. Paradoxically independent, at one with self, and able to form profound relationships because of it. More alive, awake, alert to self and others as their sense of self emerges.

Average: They become self-effacing, accommodating themselves, idealizing others and going along with their wishes too much, living through them. Accept conventional roles and expectations naively, unquestioningly. Fearing change and conflicts, they become passive and disengaged: too easygoing, phlegmatic, unresponsive, complacent, they walk away from problems, brushing them under the rug. Thinking becomes hazy and ruminative, mostly about their fantasies, as they begin to tune out reality, becoming oblivious, unreflective, and inattentive. Emotional indolence, indifference, unwillingness to exert self (and stay focused) on problems when the need arises. Begin to minimize problems to appease others and to have peace at any price. Become fatalistic and resigned, as if nothing can be done to change anything. Engage in wishful thinking, looking for quick, magical solutions.

Unhealthy: They can be too repressed, undeveloped, and ineffec-
tual. Do not want to deal with problems: become obstinate, dis-
sociating self from all conflicts. Thus, they become neglectful
and dangerous to others. Dissociate so much from anything
threatening that they eventually cannot function: become se-
verely disoriented, depersonalized, catatonic. Multiple personal-
ities are possible as extreme pathology.

See *Personality Types*, 246–73, *Understanding the Enneagram*, 76–81, and "Recommendations for Personal Growth" in
UTE, 255–57.

Personality Type One: *The Reformer*
*The Rational, Idealistic Type: Rational, Principled, Orderly,
Perfectionistic, and Intolerant*

Personality type One is the type in the Relating Triad whose
ability to relate to the environment is underdeveloped; that is,
Ones need to feel justified by their conscience before they can
act. Ones also have problems relating to people and the environment because they see themselves as needing to be perfect before
they allow themselves to do whatever they do or want whatever
they want. Ones see themselves and the world around them as
being in less than an ideal state; hence, they are unsatisfied with
reality as it is (and with themselves) since the world could always
be improved. Average to unhealthy Ones become increasingly
angry and intolerant if the environment does not obey their pre-
scriptions for perfection. Some of the major behavioral characteristics of Ones are the following.

Healthy: They are conscientious and have a strong sense of right
and wrong. Rational, reasonable, self-disciplined, mature, moderate. Extremely principled, always want to be fair and objective
with others. Ethical: truth and justice are primary values. Personal integrity and rectitude make them moral teachers and advocates for the truth. *At their best:* They become extraordinarily
wise, discerning, and tolerant. Transcendentally realistic, know-

ing the best thing to do in all circumstances. They believe that the truth will eventually be heard.

Average: They become high-minded idealists, feeling *noblesse oblige* — that it is up to them to strive to improve everything by becoming reformers, advocates, critics, and crusaders. They become involved in causes, making progress toward the ideal, toward how they think things "ought" to be. Afraid of making a mistake: everything must be consistent with their ideals. Become orderly and well organized but impersonal, too emotionally constricted, rigid and logical, keeping their feelings and impulses in tight check. Puritanical, punctual, pedantic, and fastidious. Their thinking is deductive and hierarchical, in dichotomies of black and white, right and wrong, good and bad. Very critical both of self and others: picky, judgmental, perfectionistic. Highly opinionated about everything: correcting people and badgering them to do what they think is right. Impatient, never settling for less than perfection in self and others. Moralizing, scolding, abrasive, and indignantly angry toward others if they do not do as they are told.

Unhealthy: They can be self-righteous, intolerant, highly dogmatic, and inflexible. They deal in absolutes: they alone know "the truth." Very severe in judgments toward others, although rationalizing their own actions. While obsessed about the wrongdoing of others, Ones may become contradictory and hypocritical, doing the opposite of what they preach. Become condemnatory, punitive, and cruel. Pathology seen as a serious nervous breakdown and severe depression.

See *Personality Types*, 274–301, *Understanding the Enneagram*, 81–85, and "Recommendations for Personal Growth" in *UTE*, 258–60.

SECTION 6. Interpreting the RETI

Although discovering your basic personality type is the primary objective of the RETI, you can also gain more information about your personality and its dynamics from the test.

In most cases, the highest score is your basic personality type; however, occasionally the basic type may be only two or three points higher than another type, or several types may be equal. There may also be other unusual results. This section is concerned with interpreting the RETI, particularly in cases where the results differ somewhat from what is expected.

In this section, we will discuss the nine personality types as psychological Functions operative within each of us, briefly comment on patterns and issues frequently seen with this questionnaire, and present five case studies that illustrate different aspects of interpretation.

The Functions

From one point of view, each of the personality types is a metaphor for a wide range of behaviors and attitudes, just as in astrology different "houses" denote particular areas of human activity. The nine personality types of the Enneagram can thus be regarded as psychological "functions" and "potentials for" a wide spectrum of healthy to unhealthy traits. One reason we are all similar is that all nine Functions operate in each of us; one reason we are different is that their proportion and balance within our psyches is different.

I have given two names to each Function because each personality type represents two major areas of activity — a Function that characterizes an internally held *attitude* of the type and a Function that characterizes the type's observable *behavior*. High scores in one or more of the types indicate that you have already developed the Functions or the capacities of these types, whereas relatively low scores indicate that you need to give more attention to developing these other potentials. (The following short sketches of the Functions are suggestive, not exhaustive, treatments of this aspect of the Enneagram. For more qualities associated with each type as a Function, read the descriptions provided in *Personality Types* and *Understanding the Enneagram* with this interpretation in mind.)

Understood as a series of interrelated psychological Functions, the nine personality types of the Enneagram reveal the full range of one's personality. The balance of the Functions in each person produces that person's distinctive "fingerprint" or "signature": while the basic type remains constant, the other Functions in the overall pattern change over time.

Looked at from the viewpoint of the Functions, our basic personality type can thus be seen for what it is — a dominant Function (a mode of being) around which we have organized our central response to reality — while the other eight types represent the wide range of potentials that also exist within us.

THE FEELING TRIAD

TYPE TWO. The Functions of *Empathy* and *Altruism:* the potential for other-directedness, thoughtfulness for others, genuine self-sacrifice, generosity, and nurturance. Negatively, the potential for intrusiveness, possessiveness, manipulation, and self-deception.

TYPE THREE. The Functions of *Self-Esteem* and *Self-Development:* The potential for ambition, self-improvement, personal excellence, professional competence, self-assurance, and social distinction. Negatively, the potential for pragmatic calculation, arrogant narcissism, the exploitation of others, and hostility.

TYPE FOUR. The Functions of *Self-Awareness* and *Artistic Creativity:* The potential for intuition, sensitivity, individualism, self-expression, and self-revelation. Negatively, the potential for self-absorption, self-consciousness, self-doubt, self-inhibition, and depression.

THE DOING TRIAD

TYPE FIVE. The Functions of *Open-Mindedness* and *Original Thinking:* The potential for curiosity, perceptiveness, the acquisition of knowledge, inventive originality, and technical expertise. Negatively, the potential for speculative theorizing, emotional detachment, eccentricity, social isolation, and mental projections.

TYPE SIX. The Functions of *Trust* and *Social Affiliation:* The potential for emotional bonding with others, group identification, sociability, industriousness, loyalty to others, and commitment to larger efforts. Negatively, the potential for dependency, ambivalence, rebelliousness, anxiety, and inferiority feelings.

TYPE SEVEN. The Functions of *Enthusiasm* and *Practical Action:* The potential for responsiveness, productivity, achievement, skill acquisition, and the desire for change and variety. Negatively, the potential for hyperactivity, superficiality, impulsiveness, excessiveness, and escapism.

THE RELATING TRIAD

TYPE EIGHT. The Functions of *Self-Assertion* and *Leadership:* The potential for self-confidence, self-determination, self-reliance, magnanimity, and the ability to take personal initiative. Negatively, the potential for domination of others, crude insensitivity, combativeness, ruthlessness, and megalomania.

TYPE NINE. The Functions of *Acceptance* and *Receptivity:* The potential for emotional stability, humility, unself-consciousness, emotional and physical endurance, and creating harmony with others. Negatively, the potential for passivity, disengaged emotions and attention, neglectfulness, and mental dissociation.

TYPE ONE. The Functions of *Rationality* and *Social Responsibility:* The potential for moderation, conscience, maturity, self-discipline, and delayed gratification. Negatively, the potential for rigid self-control, impersonal perfectionism, judgmentalism, self-righteousness, and intolerance.

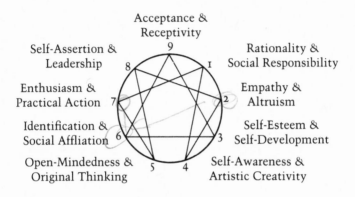

Self-Assertion &
Leadership

Enthusiasm &
Practical Action

Identification &
Social Affliation

Open-Mindedness &
Original Thinking

Acceptance &
Receptivity

Rationality &
Social Responsibility

Empathy &
Altruism

Self-Esteem &
Self-Development

Self-Awareness &
Artistic Creativity

The Enneagram of the Functions

Patterns and Issues

FLUCTUATING SCORES

If you take the RETI several times, your basic type should remain the same, although you will probably find that the scores for the other types will rise or fall depending on other influences in your life. Someone having problems with a significant relationship, for instance, is likely to register higher or lower scores in types associated with concerns about relationships, such as Two, Six, and Nine. Someone who has been putting a lot of time and energy into work or is having career problems is likely to produce elevated scores in types Three, Eight, and One. After the troubled relationship or the career issues have been resolved (one way or another), the profile for that person may change yet again. The scores for the person's basic personality type may also be affected, although the type itself will remain the same.

WINGS

Your (dominant) wing is indicated by the higher score of one of the types on either side of your basic type. For example, if you test as a Two, your wing will be One or Three, whichever has the higher score.

The second highest *overall* score on the RETI is not necessarily that of the wing. For instance, a Six's second highest score may be Nine; this does not mean that his or her wing is Nine. (Look at the scores for Five and Seven; the higher is the Six's wing.)

In all cases, the proportion of the wing to that of the basic type must be taken into consideration. Some people will have a relatively high wing score in proportion to their basic type. Some will have a moderate, or even a low, proportion of wing to basic type. This consideration is significant for understanding a person's motivations and behavior, particularly if a prediction of his or her performance is being attempted, as in a business setting. Understanding the relative proportion of the wing to the basic type also yields insights into the childhood origins of the person, codependency issues, and potential pathology. (For a complete explanation of the proportion of wing to basic type, see *PT*, 312–13.)

In some cases, the "wrong" wing will score higher than a person's actual wing (as determined by subjects themselves or by trained Enneagram judges). An anomaly such as this could result when the qualities of the basic type and the wing are in conflict. In the descriptions of the wings in *Personality Types*, I noted that some combinations of the basic type and wing reinforce each other while other combinations are in conflict. For example, many qualities of the Four and the Three are in opposition, whereas the qualities of the Four and the Five reinforce each other; this situation exists for all the types and their associated wings.

You may also get a high score in a wing other than the one you are expecting because of current factors in your life. For example, someone who had been typed both by himself and by three trained Enneagram teachers as a Seven with a Six-wing tested as a Seven with an Eight-wing. In this instance, although the RETI correctly diagnosed the subject's basic type, the wing differed from what was expected. A reasonable interpretation is that the subject is in a high-pressure, competitive field where self-confidence and initiative are crucial for success. The subject has been taking more control of his career and has been making a conscious effort to be more assertive. This, coupled with the fact that types Seven and Six are in conflict, possibly caused the subject to register more responses for the Eight than for the Six.

When assessing your wing, it is always a good idea to evaluate the test results by reading the descriptions of both wings in *Personality Types* and deciding which fits you best.

CLOSE CALLS

Occasionally, someone's results will be an almost even distribution of scores among the nine types. Of course, the highest score will usually indicate the basic personality type. However, in some rare instances, there may be a tie for the high score, and it will therefore be difficult to draw conclusions about the basic type from the evidence of the test alone. Alternatively, while one score may be higher than the others, the scores for several types may be so close that it is difficult to find easily recognizable patterns among them. For example, in a specific case, a subject scored 19 points — his highest score — in three types and 18 points in two others. (This result is discussed at greater length in Case Three in this section.)

There are two explanations for this kind of close pattern. First, the subject may have been engaged in therapy or spiritual development for many years and may have resolved the problems and conflicts of his or her personality. (As we saw in Section 1, as essence is developed, personality loses its grip; hence, the more work a person does on himself or herself, the more it eventually becomes difficult to test personality, and scores would be expected to equalize.) It should be noted, however, that very few individuals seem to have attained this degree of integration and

nonidentification with their ego. This explanation should therefore be applied rarely and with great caution.

The second explanation for a relatively close distribution of
scores is that the subject may *not* have spent much time in personal development and therefore lacks the self-knowledge necessary to take the RETI properly. (Ironically, this explanation is
the exact reverse of the first.) In this situation, the same pattern
results from the subject's identification with too many traits in-
discriminately. If this should occur, the subject's personality type
may be found by having someone who knows him or her well
take the RETI either with the person or in the person's place (as
suggested in Section 4). A subject who has obtained the same
score in several types should also carefully read the Profiles in
this book and the descriptions in *Personality Types* and *Understanding the Enneagram*, with particular attention to the types'
motivations, and then retake the test.

The personality type that most frequently encounters this
difficulty is type Nine. Nines have problems seeing themselves
because their sense of self is relatively undefined. They have
developed their capacity to be unself-conscious and receptive to
others and therefore tend to see themselves in all of the types
and in none very strongly (although there is a tendency for female
Nines to misidentify themselves as Twos, and for male Nines to
misidentify themselves as Fives; see *UTE*, 159–61 and 172–76).
Furthermore, since Nines also tend to identify strongly with others, they may mistakenly apply the personality traits of loved
ones to themselves. For example, Nines married to Fours may
register high scores in Four because of their identification with
the Four spouse, not necessarily because they have actually developed the qualities of a Four themselves.

Nines are not the only type to misidentify themselves, however. Because of a strongly held self-image, emotional needs, or
social fears, individuals of other types may have extreme difficulty seeing themselves accurately and therefore may produce
unexpected (even incorrect) test results. A Three, for example,
may test almost equally high or higher in another type because
he or she invests a great deal in projecting a particular image,

especially in his or her career. Threes who want to see themselves as entrepreneurs may test high in Eight, or as intellectuals may test high in Five, or as artists may test high in Four. Furthermore, there is a cultural tendency for females to score high in Two due to socially assigned roles. It is therefore important to read the full description of each type to understand the person's underlying motivations and attitudes to make an accurate assessment.

Beyond this, it is worth noting that while some people may identify their type correctly, they may not want to admit aspects of themselves either to themselves or to anyone else. Obviously, no test of personality can work unless subjects are willing and able to look at themselves honestly.

HIGH SCORES TOWARD UNHEALTH

High scores in a subject's Direction of Disintegration do not necessarily mean that the person is unhealthy. It is possible either that the person has integrated around the Enneagram and is developing the positive aspects of the Function that is symbolized by that type or that temporary circumstances in the person's life are eliciting aspects of the type.

The RETI does not purport to measure health or unhealth, self-actualization or pathology. The primary concern of this test is to determine your basic personality type, and any other conclusions drawn from the test are relatively speculative.

Furthermore, the statements for each type have been designed to fall within the *healthy to average* range of the Levels of Development, that is, between Levels 2 and 6 on the Continuum (see Section 1). It would therefore be virtually impossible for pathology to be discovered by this test. While high scores in the type in your Direction of Disintegration may alert you to an "unhealthy" tendency, the RETI does not diagnose neuroses or mental disorders.

Remember that if the type in your Direction of Disintegration is understood as a psychological Function, the type is part of your overall personality and, as such, must be integrated into it. All types, no matter how high or low they score on this test, must be taken into consideration.

To further analyze your scores for any type, carefully read the set of 32 statements for the type in Section 7.

Case Studies

The following brief case studies illustrate some of the principles and problems encountered in interpreting the RETI.

We will first examine a normal pattern of responses that clearly indicated the subject's basic type, wing, and Directions of Integration and Disintegration. The second case is of a subject whose results revealed an unexpectedly elevated score because of conscious efforts he had been making to change his social and economic circumstances. The third case illustrates how relatively flat responses to all nine types can make a diagnosis difficult. The fourth case illustrates the effects of pathology, and the fifth case illustrates fluctuations in the personality functions in the same person tested at different times.

Case One: A Normal Pattern

Type	Two	Three	Four	Five	Six	Seven	Eight	Nine	One
Score									
32									
31									
30					30				
25								26	
20									
		18							
15									
	14		12			14	12		
10									11
				7					
5									
	Two	Three	Four	Five	Six	Seven	Eight	Nine	One

This subject's scores are straightforward and unambiguous: the subject tested as a Six with a Seven-wing; her high score in Nine indicates that she is probably developing toward her Direction of Integration. The type in her Direction of Disintegration, Three, is also elevated, although in this case it suggests movement toward further integration around the Enneagram beyond Nine to Three, the personality function that she ultimately most needs to develop (*PT*, 307). Note that (with the exception of the Five, the intellectual component) most of this subject's other scores were fairly close to the median of 16, indicating a balance of the components of her personality. The relatively low score for Five suggests that the subject may wish to spend more time developing intellectual activities and pursuits. The subject confirmed that she is a Six with a Seven-wing and that the pattern in the chart reflects her experience of herself.

Case Two: An Unexpectedly Elevated Function

Type	Two	Three	Four	Five	Six	Seven	Eight	Nine	One
Score									
32						32			
31									
30									
25									
20		21					20		
			17	17					
15									
10					11			10	10
5	6								
	Two	Three	Four	Five	Six	Seven	Eight	Nine	One

Special circumstances may result in a high score in a type other than a subject's wing, Direction of Integration, or Direction of

Disintegration. In this case, the subject's highest score was in Seven and his second highest score was in Three. By reading the profiles and descriptions in *Personality Types*, the subject confirmed that he is a personality type Seven with an Eight-wing. This was further confirmed by the expert opinion of a trained Enneagram teacher. The subject was puzzled, however, by his high Three score since this was not the type in his Direction of Integration or Disintegration. That outcome was explained by the fact that the subject had been consciously developing himself in a number of personal and professional areas. It was therefore not surprising that Three should emerge as a high score, followed by the type in his Direction of Integration, Five.

In this particular case, not only did the RETI correctly assess the subject's basic type, wing, and Direction of Integration, the test also indicated the factor that was uppermost in the subject's mind — his personal ambition, as shown by the high score in the type Three function. Given these findings, the subject felt that the RETI accurately diagnosed his personality and current concerns.

Case Three: A Close Discrimination

The first time this subject took the test, he scored 19, 19, 18, 19, 11, 17, 18, 9, and 14 in types Two through One, respectively. Because of this unusually flat pattern of responses, the subject was urged to take the test again, and the pattern in the chart emerged. The subject had been trying to decide whether he was a personality type Four or Five, and the answer became clear, although all of his scores remained close.

As indicated by the scores in the chart, the subject tested as a Four with a Five-wing and confirmed this assessment by reading the descriptions in *Personality Types*. What helped the subject decide whether he was a Four with a heavy Five-wing or a Five with a heavy Four-wing was that in each of the four statements in which he was forced to choose between the Four and the Five, he chose the Four statement.

His flat response patterns in both tests may also have been because the subject is a therapist, has spent years in self-devel-

Case Three: A Close Discrimination

Type	Two	Three	Four	Five	Six	Seven	Eight	Nine	One
Score									
32									
31									
30									
25									
			22						
20	19			19					
		17				16	15		
15									15
					11				
10								10	
5									
	Two	Three	Four	Five	Six	Seven	Eight	Nine	One

opment, and has made conscious efforts at not identifying with his ego or personality. While this explanation is not conclusive, it suggests that some effects of spiritual development may be testable.

Case Four: The Effects of Pathology

The opinion about this subject by expert Enneagram judges was that he is a Nine with an Eight-wing. This finding was confirmed by the RETI. The outstanding feature of the profile in the chart is the subject's highly elevated score in his Direction of Disintegration, personality type Six. This finding may be due to the subject's alcoholism and feelings of self-destructiveness, low self-esteem, and dependency on his wife and family for his identity. As the chart indicates, his Two score is next highest. While this score is plausible because he is a parent and breadwinner and has identified with the helper role, the score might also reflect the fact that he feels unappreciated in his roles; an examination of his type Two responses reveals a tendency to agree with state-

Case Four: The Effects of Pathology

Type	Two	Three	Four	Five	Six	Seven	Eight	Nine	One
Score									
32									
31									
30									
25					23			24	
20	21		20						
15		15							
14						14			
10							11		
8									8
5				8					
	Two	Three	Four	Five	Six	Seven	Eight	Nine	One

ments reflecting the bottom half of his Levels of Development. His high score in Four also indicates problems with self-esteem and depression. Such a pattern, coupled with evidence of alcoholism, would probably be useful to a therapist for better understanding and treating such subjects.

Case Five: Changes in Personality Patterns over Time

The two sets of scores in this chart are for the same subject taken approximately two weeks apart; the first results are in italics, the second set plain. The single number for types Three, Five, and Eight indicate that on both tests the scores were the same.

The subject clearly tested as a Five with a Four-wing in both tests, confirmed by her reading of the descriptions in *Personality Types* and by the opinion of trained Enneagram teachers. It is worth noting that, in both instances, the type in the subject's Direction of Disintegration (Seven) was high, indicating both times a potentially unhealthy tendency toward impulsiveness

Case Five: Changes in Personality Patterns over Time

Type	Two	Three	Four	Five	Six	Seven	Eight	Nine	One
Score									
32				*32*					
31									
30									
			26						
25									
			22						
20						19			
						16			*16*
15	14	*13*			*14*				14
					12				
10	*10*								
							9	9	
5								8	
	Two	Three	Four	Five	Six	Seven	Eight	Nine	One

and emotional instability. The score in type Eight, her Direction of Integration, was low, indicating that self-assertiveness and self-confidence, among the Functions of this type, need to be strengthened. Likewise, in both tests, the subject's Nine scores were low, indicating that a lack of receptivity and openness to others is a noteworthy aspect of her personality. This finding is consistent with the fact that the subject twice tested strongly as a personality type Five and, as is characteristic of this type, is highly idiosyncratic and socially detached.

The second significant finding is that, while there were noteworthy variations in some Functions, the subject's basic personality type and the overall "shape" of her personality were similar over time. This finding, replicated by different subjects who have been tested at separate times, indicates that the basic personality type, as predicted, does not change. Various intrapsychic, interpersonal, and environmental factors, however, can cause the other components of the personality to fluctuate somewhat.

7. The Statements Arranged by Type

THE 144 forced choices in the RETI contain 288 statements, or 32 statements for each of the nine personality types.

The 32 statements for each type have been grouped here so that you can confirm your test results by seeing them together. The statements begin with those reflecting healthy attitudes and behaviors and move into those expressing average attitudes and behaviors. Note where your responses have clustered. If you agree with most of the statements in the top half of the set, it is unlikely that you are moving toward this type's Direction of Disintegration. Conversely, a majority of responses in the bottom half of the set may be an early warning signal of unhealthy tendencies that you may want to be more aware of. As mentioned earlier, there are no unhealthy (or pathological) attitudes or behaviors reflected in this questionnaire.

By my convention, we begin with type Two, proceed numerically to type Nine, and end with personality type One.

PERSONALITY TYPE TWO: *THE HELPER*

6. I tend to be sympathetic and to accept what people tell me about themselves.
118. I give people attention and nurturance.
48. I am "free-spirited" and don't like being attached to a lot of material things.
105. I prefer working to help people on a one-to-one basis.
76. I think that I am more person-oriented than goal-oriented.
114. I make friends easily and often.
72. I tend to be a warm, cheerful person who enjoys the company of others.

55. I make sure that I take time to rest and reflect.
92. I am less disciplined: I know how to be spontaneous and improvise.
136. I am emotionally demonstrative.
139. I reach out to people.
40. I feel I have to make an effort to get people to like me.
132. I find I often get attached to people.
24. I spend my time with the interpersonal and the emotional.
123. It's easy for me to tell people how special they are to me.
45. I like to share intimacies and adventures with my friends.
37. I don't want to see people suffer, so I usually jump in and help.
85. I often counsel people and give personal advice.
95. I am a soft touch for those who are down on their luck.
28. I realize that I can sometimes be rather gushy and sentimental.
47. I am more likely to flatter someone.
12. I need people to be close to me and show me affection.
69. In relationships, I expect to take care of others more than they take care of me.
127. I am able to get others to confide in me.
9. I don't like to admit it, but I get into other people's business more than I should.
100. I suppose it's true that I need to be needed — but doesn't everyone?
3. I feel good about having people depend on me.
89. I often go too far and make myself too emotionally available to people.
59. I am sometimes possessive of loved ones — I have trouble letting them be.
63. I get mad when others take for granted what I've done for them.
66. A lot of thankless tasks fall on my shoulders — I wish others would think of me for a change.
32. Unfortunately, my health problems probably come from worrying too much.

PERSONALITY TYPE THREE: *THE MOTIVATOR*

4. Others would say that I am poised and self-contained.
73. I spend much of my time developing my talents and capacities.
19. People would describe me as diplomatic, charming, and ambitious.
17. I worry that I will not live up to my potential.
76. I think that I am more goal-oriented than person-oriented.
120. I am ambitious and push myself to realize my dreams.
108. I don't depend on people: I want to do things on my own.
62. A prime motive for me is to become more outstanding and esteemed as an individual.
126. I know how to make something of myself.
54. I feel that others will think less of me if I am not distinguishing myself in some way.
33. If I had to choose between my career and my friends, I'd choose my career.
132. I find I often get competitive with people.
94. I don't like admitting it, but I often compare myself with others.
64. I need to make my own way and have trouble cooperating with others.
43. Being sympathetic is okay, but others have to take responsibility for themselves.
140. I want to be socially acceptable.
15. Much of my success has been due to my talent for making a favorable impression.
83. I am self-conscious about how I come across to people.
124. The positive feedback I get from others is important to me.
11. I am adaptable and can quickly find a way to fit into almost any situation.
35. When I run into difficulties, I change my tactics.
115. I am secretive about my private life.
137. I'm not a very easy person to get to know — I like to keep people guessing.

69. In relationships, I expect others to support me in my endeavors.
101. I enjoy talking about myself and being the center of attention.
144. I don't believe that personality questionnaires are valid because they cannot encompass the unlimited potential of human beings.
106. Having people admire me is important to me.
52. It really bothers me when others don't think well of me.
88. Privately, I think I am better than most.
80. I am sometimes hostile and dismissive.
96. Typically, when I get angry, I become distant and icy.
28. I realize that I can sometimes be rather aloof and superior.

PERSONALITY TYPE FOUR: *THE ARTIST*

1. One of my greatest assets is the depth of my feelings.
109. I am more intuitive than cerebral.
73. I spend much of my time in self-exploration.
128. I take time to figure out what my feelings and impulses are telling me.
36. In general, I am past-oriented.
50. One of my main assets is my ability to describe internal states.
30. I don't mind revealing my weaknesses to others, and often do.
81. I let others find their own way and make their own mistakes.
57. It's important to me to let others know how I feel, though I may express myself indirectly.
61. It's important to me to have an aesthetically pleasing environment.
22. I am romantic and give myself to many strong emotions.
117. I am fairly impractical and something of a dreamer.
70. In the face of adversity, I tend to escape into fantasy.
11. I stand back from new situations and it takes me a while to see if I fit in.

133. In social situations, I tend to talk intimately with one or two people or keep to myself.
123. It's difficult for me to tell people how special they are to me.
135. When I get angry at people, I find it difficult to confront them.
113. When I have conflicts with others, I tend to withdraw.
 44. I have a poetic sensibility, although that usually includes feeling lonely and emotionally vulnerable.
 86. I usually feel like an outsider.
 20. I brood about my problems until I can let them go.
 99. I tend to be moody and self-absorbed.
143. I often question myself about my motives and feelings.
104. Generally speaking, I have tended to be pessimistic.
 97. I often feel inhibited and unable to express myself well.
101. I feel uneasy talking about myself and being the center of attention.
139. I rarely reach out to people.
 88. Privately, I think I am more flawed than most.
  3. I feel uncomfortable when people depend on me.
 46. Fulfilling social obligations is not high on my agenda.
 91. I may seem to others to be self-indulgent and sensual.
 66. I sometimes hold myself back too much and am blocked from doing good things for myself.

PERSONALITY TYPE FIVE: *THE THINKER*

  1. One of my greatest assets is the sharpness of my mind.
109. I am more cerebral than intuitive.
 31. One of my deepest drives is to understand the world around me.
 79. Life can be ambiguous, but with insight you can begin to make sense of it all.
 84. I am patient: I stand back and observe things.
121. I tend to be focused and intense.
 51. People come to me because I have knowledge that they need.

8. I care less about practical results than about pursuing my inspirations.

24. I spend my time with the abstract and the mental.

38. I would sacrifice a great deal to be an expert in some field.

29. I lose track of time and work best with as little structure as possible.

75. I tend to be unconventional and idiosyncratic in many areas of my life.

15. Much of my success has been achieved despite my limited interpersonal skills.

53. I can be rather Spartan and need minimal creature comforts while I'm working.

61. Having an aesthetically pleasing environment is not a high priority for me.

10. Under pressure, I tend to detach emotionally and "go into my head."

34. I hesitate to act until I've thought through things carefully.

116. People have told me to stop considering so many alternatives and do something definite.

107. It is hard to know what to do because morality is so relative.

12. I need to maintain a certain distance with people.

136. I am not very emotionally demonstrative.

114. I don't make friends easily.

71. It's difficult for me to ask for things.

124. I know if I've done something well, and don't need the reactions of others to confirm it.

103. I have tended to avoid most physical activities.

99. I tend to be emotionally detached and preoccupied.

111. I have found that the more I reduce my needs, the simpler life becomes.

140. I care little about being socially acceptable.

144. I believe that personality questionnaires are probably valid because human behavior is rather predictable.

42. I distrust authority and ignore rules as much as possible.

90. People have said that I'm too argumentative — I guess I enjoy a good debate.

130. It makes me mad when people refuse to face unpleasant realities.

PERSONALITY TYPE SIX: *THE LOYALIST*

67. I identify strongly with others and form lasting bonds of trust and friendship.
117. I am practical and down-to-earth.
108. I depend on my friends and they know they can depend on me.
92. I am well disciplined: I know how to get organized and follow through with details.
110. I have a deep need for security.
49. I am more hard-working and responsible than many of my friends.
38. I would sacrifice a great deal to build a secure life for myself and my loved ones.
105. I prefer working with others on a team effort.
129. I function well in groups.
75. I tend to be a regular guy or gal and a traditionalist in many areas of my life.
133. In social situations, I tend to talk and banter with a lot of different people.
33. If I had to choose between my friends and my career, I'd choose my friends.
119. I am methodical and cautious.
85. I don't get too personally involved in other people's lives.
64. I need to know what's expected of me and have trouble striking out on my own.
70. In the face of adversity, I tend to "gut it out" to the bitter end.
46. I take my social obligations very seriously.
77. I stand by my friends, even if they might be wrong.
27. When I am unsure of what to do, I like to get advice from others.
138. In a difficult situation, I need reassurance from others.
21. I can assume leadership if need be, although I have problems making decisions.

14. Although I sometimes complain about it, I need pressure to get me going.
18. I watch people until I am sure they can be trusted.
59. I often don't know how I feel about others.
142. One of my fears is being taken advantage of.
5. I realize that I sometimes fret about my problems too much.
56. I tend to procrastinate and do not like taking the initiative myself.
25. People would say that I am often "uptight."
10. Under pressure, I tend to worry and react strongly.
87. It's hard for me not to complain when others don't do their jobs and put me under more pressure.
80. I am sometimes stubborn and defensive.
42. It makes me furious when others break the rules and get away with it.

PERSONALITY TYPE SEVEN: *THE GENERALIST*

121. I tend to be spontaneous and fun-loving.
41. I am like the weather: I change constantly.
68. I seek stimulation and excitement.
36. In general, I am future-oriented.
58. I am an outgoing, sociable person.
49. I am more positive and enthusiastic than many of my friends.
4. Others would say that I am vivacious and uninhibited.
103. I have tended to like most physical activities.
115. I talk openly about my private life.
13. There's a bit of the storyteller and entertainer in me.
141. I like many different things and am eager for new experiences.
134. I love having a lot of people in my life.
17. I worry that I'll miss out on the good things of life.
119. I am adventurous and take risks.
82. I use my money primarily to obtain interesting, pleasurable experiences.

125. I'm very free with money, and spend more lavishly than I should.

53. It is important for me to have my creature comforts while I'm working.

44. I am practical and have many new ideas, although I don't complete as many as I would like to.

27. When I need to make a decision, I try different things to see what works best for me.

20. I distract myself with other things until I find a way to handle my problems.

100. I suppose it's true that I am self-centered and don't like people needing me too much.

55. I don't like wasting time "doing nothing."

131. I usually follow my feelings and impulses.

39. I like "letting go" and pushing the limits.

97. I am outspoken — I say what others wish they had the nerve to say.

71. I usually make my needs known.

6. I tend to be skeptical and don't believe every story I hear.

23. I am a "stormy" person and have volatile feelings.

87. It's hard for me not to put down those who can't keep up with my pace.

94. I don't like admitting it, but I am rarely satisfied with what I have.

78. When things get to me, I make it up to myself by "going on a binge."

32. Unfortunately, my health problems probably come from going to extremes with my bad habits.

PERSONALITY TYPE EIGHT: *THE LEADER*

67. I champion others and use my resources to help them make something of themselves.

79. Life is a struggle, but with courage you can do something great.

41. I am like a rock: I'm solid and steady.

48. I am earthy and I enjoy dealing with the material world.

50. One of my main assets is my ability to take charge of situations.
118. I give people direction and motivation.
16. I persuade people with my confidence and the strength of my personality.
21. It's easy for me to assume leadership and I have little problem making decisions.
106. Having an impact on the lives of others is important to me.
34. I act quickly, confident that I can make things work out.
8. I am practical-minded and want my work to have concrete results.
62. A prime motive for me is to become more powerful and influential as an individual.
122. Generally, my actions are based on the needs of the situation.
26. In general, I put practical results over abstract "ideals."
2. Although I know how to relax, I am basically hard-driving.
82. I use my money primarily to maintain and improve my position in life.
37. I don't want to spoil people, but if they want to help themselves, I'll show them how.
125. I have worked hard for my money and keep track of it carefully.
111. I have found that the more I have, the simpler life becomes.
128. Navel-gazing is a waste of time: getting things done is what counts.
142. One of my fears is being dependent on someone else.
56. I take the initiative and don't mind pushing to get what I want.
30. I don't want to reveal my weaknesses to others, and rarely do.
98. I don't fear having conflicts with others.
74. Whether you like it or not, you have to take care of Number One first.
134. I don't need a lot of people in my life.
102. I sometimes put people off by being too forceful.

52. I don't care if others like me as long as they respect me.
89. It's hard for me to let down my guard around people — even my loved ones.
113. When I have conflicts with others, I rarely back down.
60. I tend to be confrontational.
96. Typically, when I get angry I shout and tell people off.

PERSONALITY TYPE NINE: *THE PEACEMAKER*

68. I seek contentment and "peace of mind."
23. I am a "mellow" person in whom "still waters run deep."
31. One of my deepest drives is to feel close to others.
104. Generally speaking, I have tended to be optimistic.
86. I usually feel comfortable around people.
65. When I meet people, I come across as having a sunny, casual disposition.
45. I like to relax and unwind with friends.
2. Although I can be ambitious, I am basically easygoing.
137. I'm like an open book — "what you see is what you get."
40. People seem to naturally like me.
51. People come to me because I make them feel safe and appreciated.
60. I tend to be self-effacing.
43. I usually sympathize with the other person's point of view.
112. I am less perfectionistic — getting along with people is more important to me.
74. Those who think only of themselves first will end up lonely and unhappy.
120. I am not very ambitious for myself, but I work hard for my loved ones.
7. Why focus on the negative when there is so much that's wonderful about life?
18. I am very open to people and am surprised if they turn out different from what I thought.
57. It's not always important to me to tell others how I feel.
5. I realize that I sometimes avoid thinking about my problems too much.

14. I don't handle pressure well, and work best at my own pace.
93. I realize that sometimes I am too complacent and a day-dreamer.
141. I know what I like, so why waste my time trying something I might not like?
127. What people do is their own business and it doesn't concern me.
83. I am not particularly self-conscious when I am around people.
143. I seldom question myself about my motives and feelings.
25. People would say that I am often "spaced out."
90. People have said that I'm too accommodating — I just don't like arguing.
98. I fear having conflicts with others.
9. I don't like to admit it, but I let little problems go until they become big ones.
130. It makes me mad when people try to upset me about things I can't do anything about.
78. When things get to me, I am able to "tune them out."

PERSONALITY TYPE ONE: *THE REFORMER*

65. When I meet people, I come across as having a mature, dignified nature.
131. I usually follow my conscience and reason.
16. I persuade people with my honesty and the reasonableness of my arguments.
58. I am an earnest, self-disciplined person.
72. I tend to be a serious, reserved person who likes discussing issues.
138. In a difficult situation, I am usually sure of where I stand.
19. People would describe me as direct, formal, and idealistic.
122. Generally, my actions are based on principles.
110. I have a strong need to feel that I am right.
126. I know the right way to live.
13. There's a bit of the teacher and crusader in me.

7. I don't like being critical, but I can't help noticing when things are wrong.
84. I am impatient: I jump in and attack problems.
135. When I get angry at people, I let them know what is on my mind.
129. I find it frustrating to function in groups.
26. In general, I put my ideals over obtaining practical "results."
35. When I run into difficulties, I try harder.
54. I feel that I am slacking off if I am not making progress.
116. People have told me that I need to relax and enjoy life for a change.
77. I will not compromise myself for friendship.
29. I am very conscious of time and need structure to get things done.
39. I find I don't like losing control of myself very much.
22. I am logical and don't like getting too emotional.
91. I may seem to others to be impersonal and self-controlled.
95. There are proper channels to which a needy person can apply for help.
102. I sometimes put people off by being too impersonal.
81. I think it's better to help others see that they are making a mistake.
107. It is not hard to know what to do because moral truth is self-evident.
63. I get mad when others do not follow my instructions more carefully.
47. I am more likely to criticize someone.
93. I realize that sometimes I am too judgmental and impatient.
112. I am a perfectionist and I push to get things done right, even if it makes people uncomfortable.

SECTION **8.** Enneagram
Interpretations
and Contributions

Transmission and Development

The origin of the Enneagram is a mystery and, like all good mysteries, it has kept most of its secrets to itself. Its transmission and development in more recent times, however, are somewhat less mysterious.

The two major figures in the Enneagram's modern development are George Ivanovitch Gurdjieff (c. 1877–1949) and Oscar Ichazo (b. 1931). Both have said that the Enneagram came from the Islamic brotherhoods, the Sufis, and has been passed on orally from master to disciple. They both also believed the Enneagram to be very old, possibly dating to 2500 B.C. or even earlier. (*Enneagram* is a Greek word: *ennea* means "nine," and *gram* comes from "graphein," meaning "to write"; hence, the Enneagram is a "nine-figure" or "nine-diagram.")

The first to bring the Enneagram to the West was Gurdjieff, although he never revealed precisely where he discovered it. Since Gurdjieff's death, there have been many speculations about the Enneagram's origins but little or no evidence to support them. While the Enneagram's structure seems to be related to Pythagorean number theory and to Arabic advances in mathematics — and therefore is presumably ancient — there seems to be no reason to doubt that Gurdjieff was introduced to the Enneagram by a Sufi brotherhood, the Naqshbandis, as has been claimed. However, what use the Sufis made of the Enneagram, whether their understanding of the nine personality types was the same as ours, how Gurdjieff was initiated into this secret body of knowledge, what Gurdjieff added to it himself from his extensive travels in search of ancient wisdom, and many other questions, remain unanswered and are probably unanswerable.

We know with certainty that Gurdjieff taught his students about their "Chief Feature" (a manifestation of a person's particular Capital Sin); he also specified which of the various types of "idiots" each of them was. While Gurdjieff's applications clearly indicate that he understood "personality types," it is not clear whether Gurdjieff employed the Enneagram in his teaching of them. Written evidence indicates that he probably did not. If he did, it is peculiar that his students who have written about The Work (as the Gurdjieff system is known) would have omitted this important application of the Enneagram from their many books.

Since this remarkable symbol has, until relatively recently, been transmitted only *orally*, it is not surprising that it has not been found in either written Islamic sources or in esoteric literature. It would also be surprising if either Gurdjieff or Ichazo had invented the Enneagram himself since neither has claimed to have done so and since the Enneagram has the quality of "something discovered rather than invented" (*PT*, 342). This symbol has a timeless universality about it, and a psychological typology based on it is but one of its many meanings and uses.

ALTHOUGH Gurdjieff was the first westerner to have transmitted the Enneagram from the Middle East, credit for important early work on it goes to the Bolivian mystic and teacher Oscar Ichazo, the founder of the Arica Institute. Ichazo says that he discovered the Enneagram during his travels in Afghanistan in the sixties; he also claims that much of his understanding of the Enneagram was revealed to him in a trance before he studied Gurdjieff's system. While Ichazo's work is impressive and intriguing, it is a synthesis of concepts drawn from Eastern Orthodox Christianity, Buddhism, the Cabala, Hinduism, mysticism, and Western esotericism, making his teaching (of which the Enneagram is only a part) somewhat obscure to most westerners. Ichazo has also been secretive about his interpretation of the Enneagram and has, to date, revealed his understanding of it primarily to his own students.

Ichazo began teaching the Enneagram as part of his school for human transformation (Arica) first in Arica, Chile, and later in the United States after founding the Arica Institute in 1970. One of his students, the psychiatrist Claudio Naranjo, learned the Enneagram from Ichazo and began teaching it in California shortly after his return from Chile. Since Ichazo has not written in much detail about his interpretation of the Enneagram except in Arica training manuals, it is difficult to evaluate his discoveries fully. It is also difficult to sort out the contributions made solely by Ichazo from those made by Naranjo. Since Naranjo is a noted psychiatrist and writer, it is reasonable to believe that Naranjo was the first to give the Enneagram a distinctly "psychological" interpretation, although until Ichazo produces an account of his development of the Enneagram for the reading public, this remains to be seen.

Despite the major seminal discoveries and contributions of Ichazo and Naranjo, the Enneagram remained in a somewhat ambiguous state in the early 1970s since the "Arica tradition" (as I have named this interpretation of the Enneagram) was taught confidentially only in Arica schools and therefore did not have the benefit of either scholarly or public examination. Furthermore, Ichazo and Naranjo soon broke off relations, and on his return to the United States Naranjo began teaching his "unauthorized" version of the Enneagram to his own students.

One of them was the Jesuit priest Robert Ochs, who transmitted Naranjo's interpretation to other Jesuit priests and seminarians around North America. They in turn made use of it for spiritual counseling and added their insights to the steadily growing and constantly changing core of material. The "Jesuit tradition" is thus an offshoot of the "Naranjo tradition"; both are offshoots of the original "Arica tradition" and are somewhat different from it.

When I encountered the Jesuit tradition of the Enneagram in Toronto in 1973 as a Jesuit seminarian, it consisted of nine one-page impressionistic descriptions of the personality types along with several pages of Enneagrams labeled with the names of the ego fixations, the passions, the virtues, the traps, and other material that had been transmitted more or less intact from the Arica tradition. The Jesuit tradition also included an "oral tradition" of its own, some of which made sense, some of which did not. Thus, even in the early seventies, confusion was setting in — and more was to follow — as claims began to be made about what constituted the "authentic teaching."

Unfortunately, confusion and misinformation about the Enneagram have been part of the picture from the beginning of its public dissemination in North America because few had access to the Arica material and those who did were sworn to secrecy. For those working in the Jesuit tradition, the fear of provoking a lawsuit for copyright infringement by using Arica's materials without permission prevented them from publishing their notes and observations about the personality types. A public debate about the relative merits of the various interpretations that were developing seemed hopeless, or at best a distant hope.

A more fundamental reason for confusion was that little of the theory of the Enneagram or of the descriptions of the types had been worked out, at least in the Naranjo and Jesuit traditions. Since everything was sketchy and somewhat clandestine, no one knew with any assurance which interpretation was "right," where anything came from, or who had contributed what. Ironically, rather than simply observe human nature to answer questions of interpretation, many in the Jesuit tradition began to treat the Enneagram as if it were another dogma to be believed unquestioningly rather than as the living, experiential thing it is.

These problems with the transmission of the Enneagram have taken their toll, and their damage can still be felt today. Confusion about many aspects of the Enneagram's history, development, and transmission are still widespread. How the personality types themselves are conceived is also confused because, ironically, many generalizations about the types can be made and still seem plausible. There is enough elasticity and ambiguity in human nature to disguise a fair amount of lazy thinking and poor scholarship without being detected easily. Nevertheless, despite the misinformation flying around in the mid-seventies — and remaining today — the Enneagram has a ring of truth about it. The seminal insights of Ichazo and Naranjo into the nine personality types revealed a profound understanding of human nature, one that appealed instantly to a broad spectrum of people.

AS IMPORTANT as the early work on the Enneagram had been, I felt that if this system was to have the impact it seemed to deserve, it would have to be improved in many areas, primarily in the descriptions of the nine types. One could see that mistakes about the types were being taught: some of the types as a whole were too limited and distorted to account for the vast diversity of human beings; traits had been mistakenly assigned from one type to another; important elements were missing, such as a description of the *healthy* side of each type. Even though the early Enneagram was fascinating, it was also disappointing in its incompleteness, inconsistencies, and internal contradictions. The system needed an overhaul.

On September 2, 1975, I began full-time work on the Enneagram, interpreting the Jesuit tradition in the light of Freud, Jung, Karen Horney, Erich Fromm, and other modern psychologists. Because I had been introduced to the Enneagram in the Jesuit tradition, I continued to work in it, although I eliminated the overtly religious tone and content of that interpretation. I was and am convinced that the Enneagram is neither primarily religious in nature nor merely another psychological typology, but an all-encompassing psychology of personality that, among other things, has profound spiritual implications.

I was greatly aided by my then naive belief that problems with the Enneagram could be solved quickly and that comprehensive, self-evidently accurate descriptions of the types could be produced. That I did not subscribe to any "school" of psychology proved to be a blessing since I was not unduly influenced by a particular point of view — and, more important, I was not discouraged by the prevailing academic opinion that the task I had undertaken was virtually impossible: working out descriptions of universally applicable personality types and discovering their inner mechanics — why they are as they are — is the stuff of age-old fantasies. This was best left to geniuses or madmen. Since I was neither and was working alone and could call only on my own observations, intuitions, and reading, the task seemed doomed from the start.

In the end, my ignorance of what was possible protected me from feeling the full impact of what I had undertaken until I was a few years into my work and realized how vast the task was. But by then I had committed myself to the project and had made several discoveries that allowed me to add fresh material and organize it in a new way. For instance, it is likely that, if I had not discovered the Levels of Development in July 1977, to cite one central innovation, it would have been impossible for me to carry on. But once I had made it, the discovery carried me forward. I am grateful that it did.

IT IS IMPORTANT for everyone interested in the Enneagram to understand that significant differences in interpretation exist among the available Enneagram books. While each has been written from a different point of view and adds certain new insights, much is contradictory and inaccurate. The results you obtain with the *Riso Enneagram Type Indicator* may therefore be different from the assessment you may have made of your personality type based on descriptions found in other books.

For example, you may believe that you are a certain type because you have read other Enneagram books or because you have been "typed" by an Enneagram teacher. The RETI, however, may indicate that you are another type altogether. To find out which type you actually are, please carefully read the full description in *Personality Types* for the type assessed by the RETI to see if it actually fits you better than the type with which you have previously identified.

Readers should be aware that significant contradictions and incompatibilities exist among the Enneagram books because they do not all describe the personality types in the same way. Many contain misconceptions about the types as a whole (for instance, Eights and Ones, Nines and Fives, Fours and Fives, and

Threes and Sevens are often confused). Several books also contain misattributions of traits from type to type, mistaken psychiatric correlations, and misassessments of examples of famous people used to illustrate the types. (For example, Mikhail Gorbachev is listed by some as a type One, Elizabeth Taylor as a type Two, Ronald Reagan as a type Three, and Bette Davis as a type Four. These assessments are far off the mark, and there are many similar mistakes.) Inaccuracies of this kind are particularly telling since they inadvertently reveal an inadequate understanding of the personality types themselves. Likewise, others have attempted to produce an Enneagram questionnaire for some time but have been unable to do so because, it seems to me, their underlying conception of the types is confused and distorted.

Naturally, my own books, including this questionnaire, reflect my evolving understanding of the Enneagram and of human nature. (And like the other books, mine may also contain some mistakes.) Anyone seriously interested in the Enneagram is urged to think critically and to test the validity of the various interpretations for themselves.

A GREAT deal of confusion also exists concerning the contributions made by different authors. Misunderstandings about this have been somewhat understandable since, as noted earlier, the Enneagram was disseminated in the seventies by enthusiasts passing around photocopied notes from the Arica and Jesuit traditions. These notes were usually not attributed to anyone, and so it was extremely difficult to know who had authored them. As books began to be published, some clarity began to emerge, but even so, many assumed that everything about the Enneagram belonged to an ancient oral tradition and was therefore in the public domain — or, worse, that everyone was borrowing from everyone else and that no one had done any original work in the field.

This is certainly not the case, and as the Enneagram becomes better known, it is all the more necessary to have a clearer idea of the origins of the various interpretations now in circulation.

Unfortunately, we will have to wait for an independent, critical history of the Enneagram to be written for all of the claims and counterclaims to be adequately sorted out. Until someone undertakes to produce such a book, Enneagram writers have an obligation to inform their readers about which tradition they are working in, where they have obtained their material, how they have developed it, and what contributions they themselves have made.

In an attempt to fulfill these obligations, I previously stated that "everything in *Personality Types* and in [*Understanding the Enneagram*] that has not been explicitly attributed to someone else or to a specific traditional source is the result of my original work" (*UTE*, 17). I then made a few comments about how I discovered the Levels of Development and the childhood origins of the types and produced my own type names and so forth, without, however, providing a complete list of all my discoveries "for the record." I believed that this general statement would be enough to clarify what I had contributed to the development of the Enneagram.

I was wrong. My publisher, Houghton Mifflin, and I are therefore taking the opportunity provided by the publication of this book to set forth my discoveries. Almost all of them have, to date, been published either in *Personality Types* or in *Understanding the Enneagram*. With the exception of the "Psychic Structures" (number 10 in the following list), most of them have either been mentioned or implied in these two books. However, not all of them were taught explicitly: *Personality Types* contains a great deal of information "in between the lines" — for instance, the defense mechanisms, the Basic Fears, and the Basic Desires for the types are given in each description, although without being specified directly. (In *Understanding the Enneagram*, I was explicit about more material and will be even more explicit in future books.)

With apologies for the immodesty of the following list — but with the hope that readers will understand its necessity — the following are among my contributions to Enneagram theory and practice.

1. The complete *systematic description* of each of the nine personality types. Clarifying and elaborating the impressionistic sketches from the Jesuit tradition to detailed descriptions of approximately 10,000 words for each type found in *Personality Types.*

2. The nine *Levels of Development* within each personality type and how they are structured into healthy, average, and unhealthy areas of functioning; the internal symmetries between the Levels, and the 81 descriptive titles given to each Level ("The Inspired Creator" and "The Self-Aware Intuitive" for personality type Four, and so forth, for all the types).

3. The developmental *Childhood Origins* for each type and how they are responsible for each type's basic motivations, sense of self, cognitive style, and overall pattern of traits. (More about this will be published in the forthcoming *Working with the Enneagram.*)

4. The *Basic Fear* and *Basic Desire* for each type and how the effects of these primary motivations continue to be felt in the subsequent *secondary motivations* (fears and desires) at each Level of Development for each type.

5. The most comprehensive published explanations for and descriptions of the *Direction of Integration* and *Direction of Disintegration* for each type, thus revealing a dynamic, predictive quality to the Enneagram.

6. The elucidation of the *full range of traits for each type,* adding hundreds of observations per type to the existing sketches in the Jesuit material. Of special note, the discovery and development of the *healthy* traits for each type, thus overcoming one of the main criticisms of the Arica and Jesuit interpretations, namely, that they were too negative.

7. The *structural interrelationships* between the personality types (such as "reversals," "foreshadowings," the "Functions," and other internal connections, most of which will be published in *Working with the Enneagram*). Demonstrating the internal coherence of the personality types indicates the subtlety, sophistication, and complexity of the Enneagram as a multi-dimensional system.

8. The introduction of numerous changes in the *terminology* used to describe the types ("Directions of Integration and Disintegration," the "Relating Triad," "basic type," "primary" and "secondary" types, "characteristic temptation," and "saving grace," among other new terms). Similarly, producing the most appropriate, *positive descriptive labels* for the types as a whole: "The Reformer" for the One, "The Helper" for the Two, "The Motivator" for the Three, and so forth.

9. The descriptions of and rationale for the *wing* of each type, including the irregular relationship of the wing(s) to the basic type (that is, that some are in conflict with the basic type, while others reinforce the basic type). Also, the *dynamics of the wings* — how they integrate and evolve, as does the basic personality type.

10. The *Psychic Structures* for each type. The Psychic Structures (to be published in *Working with the Enneagram*) are abstract models indicating the psychological activities that occur at each Level of Development for each type.

11. The full list of *defense mechanisms* associated with each personality type. There are at least three distinct yet interrelated defense mechanisms for each type, as listed in *Understanding the Enneagram*, 44–85.

12. How the personality types of the Enneagram (properly delineated) correspond with the *psychiatric personality disorders* as well as other classification systems (Freud, Jung, Horney, Fromm, the *DSM*-III(R); for example, correspondence of Horney's aggressive, compliant, and withdrawn types to types Three, Seven, and Eight; One, Two, and Six; and Four, Five, and Nine, respectively. Correspondences to the Myers-Briggs typology will be given in *Working with the Enneagram*.)

13. Numerous *new features* and teaching aids, including the short profiles found in *PT* and *UTE* as well as this book; the recommendations for personal growth, the abstract structural patterns of each type; how the types relate to each other (to be published in *Working with the Enneagram*); and practical business applications of the Enneagram (that will be

available to my students as *The Enneagram Management Manual*).

Despite these discoveries, my understanding of human nature is still only beginning to unfold. This is, indeed, a life's work worth doing. I not only have much to learn but also much for which to give thanks, especially to those ancient masters who have handed down to us the profound wisdom of the Enneagram.

SECTION 9. A Note on Validation

THE *Riso Enneagram Type Indicator* is subject to ongoing research and field testing and will be revised in subsequent printings as necessary. Preliminary validation studies prior to publication indicate that the RETI is 85 to 90 percent accurate for identifying a person's basic personality type. This finding has been determined by correlating the questionnaire results with the subjects' assessment of their type as well as with the assessment of one or more expert Enneagram judges.

Qualified individuals who wish to conduct validation studies on the *Riso Enneagram Type Indicator* are invited to contact the author at Enneagram Personality Types, Inc., 222 Riverside Drive, Suite 10E, New York, New York, 10025.

To obtain multiple copies of *Personality Types* (1987), *Understanding the Enneagram* (1990), and *Discovering Your Personality Type: The Enneagram Questionnaire* (1992) for use in Enneagram Workshops, as well as business and organizational settings, please contact Houghton Mifflin Company, 2 Park Street, Boston, Massachusetts 02108, attention Maire Gorman, or telephone (617) 725-5969. Special discounts are available.

To contact Don Richard Riso for information about his Enneagram Workshops, professional trainings, new publications, and business seminars, or to have your name added to our mailing list for Workshops in your area, please contact Enneagram Personality Types, Inc., at the address below.

For personal consulting or to have the *Riso Enneagram Type Indicator* interpreted by an Enneagram teacher trained and certified by Don Richard Riso, please contact Enneagram Personality Types, Inc., for a referral to a teacher in your area.

For a free brochure of Enneagram Designs products, call (800) 852-9704. Outside the United States, call (803) 548-1110.

Enneagram Personality Types, Inc.
222 Riverside Drive, Suite 10E
New York, New York 10025
(212) 932-3306